Trust or Doubt

ESSENTIAL STRATEGIES TO CO-CREATE
THRIVING TEACHING TEAMS

Anabel Jensen, Ph.D.
Kathleen Gibbons, M.A.

Next Steps Press

Katy!
Welcome to NS.
I'm thrilled that
the Barber-Gibbons
Family continues to expand
& I hope that you thrive
as you co-create
the ideal that you
them intend.
♡ Katie Gibbons

Published by Next Steps Press
www.trustordoubt.com

Book Layout ©2013 BookDesignTemplates.com
Book cover by Blue Macaroon Design
Photographs courtesy of Yun Suh

Available from Amazon.com and other retail outlets.
Trust or Doubt: Essential Strategies to Co-Create Thriving Teaching Teams/ Anabel L. Jensen and Kathleen Gibbons. — 1st ed.
ISBN 978-0-692-82210-4

Contents

Dedicated to the educators who strive and work every day to enable others to succeed.

PREFACE

Our future lies not in competition, but in
responsible interdependent cooperation.

—Joseph Rain

Conflict is inevitable in a high stress, high stakes, and fast-paced profession such as teaching. Having worked in education for over 45 years, as a classroom teacher, administrator, professor, co-founder of independent schools, and consultant to private, public, and charter schools, I have faced every imaginable interpersonal conflict. *How* one responds to the conflict and resolves it with others makes all the difference in the final result. Since our society often rewards competition over cooperation, we end up with a winner-loser model of relating to each other. Consequently, the conflict often does not resolve until one person or argument wins while the other loses. In this setup, trust tends to plummet within a group, along with productivity.

Recognizing the damaging social impact of the competition-driven model, I shifted the winner-loser paradigm to a win-win framework while serving fourteen years as the principal at The Nueva School — a pioneer in social and emotional education. The collaborative win-win model proved to be the most empathic, supportive, and effective approach in resolving conflict long-term. I was gifted with many opportunities to experiment with various conflict resolution strategies as students were often sent to my office to reconcile their disagreements.

One notable instance involved two eight-year-old boys who poked, prodded, and one-upped each other repeatedly during class. It soon escalated to the students whacking each other with tree branches during recess. When they were sent to my office, the boys blamed each other for their violent and harmful behavior. To first interrupt their pattern of blaming, I asked each student to tell me the color of my office. One boy, who I will call Jake, said it was orange. The other student, who I will call Max, said it was cream colored. I informed the students that both of their responses were valid, from their vantage points. My office was painted two different colors: Jake faced the two walls that were colored orange while Max faced the two walls that were colored cream, hence the two distinct yet equally valid responses. Once the students recognized that there could be two varying perceptions of a particular situation, they were able to articulate their interaction from their own point-of-view and stop blaming each other. Max confessed that he was trying to get Jake's attention and simply stated, "I want him to play with me and spend time with me." Jake was taken aback by Max's admission because he did not recognize his desire for friendship at all. Instead, Jake felt hurt by Max "making fun of him and being mean." To transform Max's competitive approach to bonding, I assigned Max and Jake to perform two conscious acts of kindness for each other, with the only caveat that it could not involve money.

When I checked in with them at the end of the week, Max reported that Jake shared his lunch with him. Jake said that Max stayed behind to help him clean the classroom and carried his heavy bag to the bus for him. Over their school years, Jake and

Max continued to help each other and they became very good friends until they graduated together, three years later.

A win-win scenario ultimately generates and maintains a trusting relationship. Creating a win-win framework where each person feels heard and validated, and therefore is excited to move forward together and able to experience the benefits of collaboration, requires a sustained effort and considerable trial and error. Nonetheless, the work involved is worth the commitment because trust is the byproduct. A team cannot function without trust.

I am thrilled to share the strategies and trade secrets in facilitating relationships, which I have developed through training over 15,000 teachers, students, and parents at universities, K-12 schools, and workshops. It has been my greatest honor and joy to teach and learn from educators around the world so that we can contribute to the creation of trust-generating communities where everyone has a chance to thrive.

Love,
Anabel

Gettin' good players is easy.
Gettin' 'em to play together is the hard part.

—Casey Stengel

There are several helpful books on different structures of teaching teams and strategies for co-instruction (e.g., Beninghof, 2012[1]). However, there is a dearth of resources on how to best co-create and negotiate the interpersonal processes that engender a solid and high-functioning team. This is the book that I wish I had when I began my teaching career more than 15 years ago because the success of the class often depends on the quality of the team teaching relationship. Yet, in all the various teaching trainings I have received over the years, I was never modeled how to develop an effective partnership. Instead, I was placed in a teaching team, much like an arranged marriage, and was expected to know how to successfully navigate the intense working relationship. I dove into the partnership without any preparation or time to understand my co-teacher and their[*] perspective. I focused on delivering good curriculum and blindly trusted that it would all work out somehow. I assumed that we shared common goals in helping students grow. Not surprisingly, managing complicated interpersonal differences and conflicts proved to be far more time-consuming and emotionally draining than I anticipated. If I had the tactics we are about to outline in this book, I would have been able to avoid the emotional rollercoaster, better leverage my partner's and my own strengths, teach with ease, and free up so much of

---

[*]*Their, they,* or *them* is used as a singular third person pronoun throughout the book to be inclusive of non-binary gender individuals.

my emotional attention to better focus on the students' needs and classroom instruction.

The need for *TRUST or DOUBT* became more evident when I was hired to head a new K-8 school. I quickly recognized myself as the lead trust-builder in my role as an administrator in establishing the school culture. I had the privilege of managing a team that consisted of exceptional teachers from around the country. None of the teachers had ever worked together, nor had they worked in close teaching pairs. The teachers had been star educators in their previous schools and were excited to take on the challenge of opening a new school. During our first year, each teaching team had difficulty empathizing with each other's point-of-view and neglected to try on each other's methods, even if they liked each other on a personal level and got along socially. As a result, the teachers easily became frustrated during disagreements or would avoid them altogether until it became unworkable. Consequently, they had trouble delivering their curriculum together and managing their students. Seeing interpersonal challenges surface and impede the progress of talented educators motivated me to investigate the making of successful teams.

I teamed up with my former manager and mentor, Dr. Anabel Jensen, who has long modeled successful co-creative relationships in her academic, business, and writing endeavors. We got busy researching the principles of win-win teams. We also devised a survey on working in teaching teams and distributed it to a wide range of educators. In analyzing the survey responses that we sent out to a wide range of educators on working in teaching teams, we identified trust as the essential glue of a relationship. Without trust, the partnership would inevitably fall apart and at least one member would leave the team. We then distilled the key pillars that lay the groundwork for trust and their corresponding exercises. We recognized that trust is fragile and could easily be threatened with a misstep. Therefore, we also outlined all the pitfalls that break trust and cast doubt in the relationship as well as remedies to restore it.

Before the start of the academic year, we piloted our *TRUST or DOUBT* program to a group of educators who teach in teams. The training proved to be more impactful than expected. The teachers stated that the training, which they deemed as very powerful and helpful, enabled them to routinely engage in meaningful and vulnerable conversations with their teammates that were intended to help each other grow and improve. Each team also reported significantly more satisfaction and trust in their partner than their previous year. Furthermore, the participants said that their teams felt more aligned on their goals and supported by their partners. It was not perfect but overall, the teachers said that the team dynamic was almost a non-issue the year following the *TRUST or DOUBT* training, compared to their previous year.

I am elated to discover that the interpersonal issues that could block the teachers' and ultimately the students' potential could be prevented with a few days of intensive training using key tools that can create effective partnerships throughout the year. We are excited to share our insights and strategies to help remove many of the pain points of team teaching and enable educators to move eagerly forward and focused together to fulfill our great responsibility of educating young minds.

In team we trust,
Katie

INTRODUCTION

The ability to establish, grow, extend, and restore trust is the key professional and personal competency of our time.

—Stephen R. Covey

What is the most important characteristic in a team member? Participants in three studies considered various characteristics for ideal members in interdependent groups (e.g., work teams, family, athletic teams) and relationships (e.g., co-workers). Across different measures of trait importance for various groups and relationships, trustworthiness was ranked as extremely important.[2] Moreover, Harvard Business School professor and social psychologist Amy Cuddy says that trustworthiness is the *most* important factor in a professional context in how people initially assess others. While competence is highly valued, Cuddy says that it is evaluated only after trust is established.[3]

The importance of trust in groups has been documented by researchers over the years (e.g., Golembiewski and McConkie, 1975[4]; Kramer, 1999[5]). Interpersonal trust is foundational to building a climate of team psychological safety where members are comfortable being themselves and taking risks, and thereby increase learning behavior (e.g., share information, seek help, give feedback, experiment), which allows the group to adapt and improve.[6] Furthermore, psychological safety was revealed to be the most important factor in Google's multi-year internal study into the makings of a successful team.[7]

Similarly, after surveying K-8 teachers working in three different schools on effective and ineffective team teaching strategies and collaboration, we have identified trust as the glue of the relationship and the characteristic they most valued in their teammate.

In addition, there is increasing evidence (e.g., Bryk and Schneider, 2002[8]; Pil and Leana, 2009[9]) that schools with high "relational trust" - positive social relationships among members of the school community - particularly among teachers, are more likely to improve students' academic achievement. In short, a team cannot function successfully and grow without trust.

Definition of Trust

There are many definitions of trust available. We define trust as the belief that other people will respond or execute an action in a way that meets *your* expectation. It is *your* expectations along standards that we have categorized into five distinct pillars, which will be outlined shortly, that build the groundwork for trust. In other words, trust is not objective but a very subjective experience that is gauged by one's perception on distinct standards.

Trust is not an inborn trait and it is not elusive. It has concrete attributes that can be improved upon with learnable and repeatable actions. So, how can teachers establish this important bond of trust with their colleagues when they are assigned into an arranged working relationship with a virtual stranger without significant guidelines or support for creating an effective team?

From our survey among K-8 educators who work in teaching teams, key factors emerged that comprise the building blocks of trust. We then synthesized and distilled these factors to create an acronym to facilitate long-term memory. The acronym is TRUST:

Target

Recognize

Unlock

Support

Transfer

Target refers to aligning goals despite possible pedagogical and personality differences.

Recognize involves knowing one's own and teammate's recurring patterns of thoughts, feelings, and actions in order to better understand and support each other.

Unlock requires flexibility, optimism, and a growth mindset to maximize each other's potential.

Support reminds one to prioritize relationship-building and care to facilitate a teammate's growth.

Transfer refers to sharing knowledge and skills to help one's teammate to thrive.

In the upcoming chapters, the acronym of TRUST will be defined in detail, along with relevant case studies and exercises. The names of the teachers identified in the case studies have been changed, but the situations and the dynamics depicted derive from real events. The practices offered in this book are applicable to any co-teaching model (e.g., parallel, alternative, station, team teaching), and in general, any work team.

Trust requires much effort and time to build and only a matter of seconds to lose. Mishaps and obstacles that surface cannot be ignored because they could potentially break trust and cause significant damage. Therefore, each chapter also includes a common pitfall that erodes trust and casts doubt in the relationship. The pitfalls have been placed into the acronym DOUBT:

Defy

Overlook

Undermine

Belittle

Trample

Defy refers to resisting and challenging one's partner as being wrong.

Overlook involves dismissing a co-workers' needs and contributions.

Undermine creates a superior-inferior power dynamic by disapproving or weakening a partner's efforts and position, often subtly or unknowingly, while inflating one's own.

Belittle refers to overtly diminishing a partner's value and participation to the point where the teammate feels threatened.

Trample occurs when one dominates over a partner and seizes control of the team.

As the stress and needs of the students and classroom management multiply and intensify during the year, it is easy to fall into the trap of blaming one another and allowing disagreements to overwhelm the team dynamic. Even well-intentioned people can slip into damaging patterns, and thereby disrupt trust in the relationship. To prevent the negative downward spiral in the relationship, each definition of a pitfall is followed by remedies to restore trust. These action steps will help to identify destructive behavior, de-escalate conflicts, and better manage the team relationship.

To recap, each chapter begins with the definition of a key pillar for establishing trust. This is followed by a case study and various exercises to establish the foundation of trust. To prevent the team from deteriorating, a common pitfall that erodes trust is also identified and defined. This is followed by a cautionary case study. Then each chapter concludes with antidotes for the pitfall so that the team can quickly recover and restore trust.

After TRUST and DOUBT are understood and the exercises have been practiced, the Trust Factor Assessment in Chapter 6 is taken by the members of the team. This evaluation is designed to gauge the health of the team and identify areas for growth.

It is highly recommended to conduct the TRUST exercises prior to the beginning of the school year, or at the beginning of a working relationship, so that the team can launch in alignment rather than sort through interpersonal conflicts while simultaneously working to deliver the curriculum content to students. Moreover, building a strong foundation of trust in the beginning will make it much easier to resolve disagreements and differences that may arise later on.

The book's content is not devised to judge and label one's team member, since the authors believe one can only control and change oneself. In addition, it is recommended to read the book and execute the exercises together as a team, especially since most of the practices require all the team members to participate.

Here's to creating teams we can trust.

Good teams become great ones when the members trust each other enough to surrender the me for the we.

—Phil Jackson

CHAPTER 1

⊤ARGET

*When there is alignment and understanding,
it is much easier to navigate forward together,
moving in and out of agreement.*

—Karen Kimsey-House

Imagine running a morning circle meeting with students where one day, Teacher Lisa shares jokes to start the day laughing. The next day, Teacher George begins the morning meeting by reviewing the homework from the previous day. The two teachers are working towards divergent goals: Lisa aims to first emotionally connect with students to better engage the children's minds to learning. In contrast, George immediately dives into academics to quickly transition from home to school and devote every minute of their limited time to serious study. As a result of their differing objectives, the students are left confused, torn, and frustrated as to how to best begin their school day. Neither of the teacher's goals is successfully achieved.

One may believe that it would be much easier to make decisions, organize a curriculum, and operate a classroom if these two teachers came from the same background and adhered to similar methods. However, this uniformity would stifle creativity and ingenuity. New research reveals that companies with diversity (inborn and acquired) out-innovate and out-perform others.[10] It is advantageous and often the case that teaching teams are comprised of members operating from different pedagogical practices, abilities, and personalities. So how can educators' differences be leveraged as a team's strength rather than a weakness?

The problem does not reside in varied backgrounds and methods. The dilemma lies in misalignment of goals. Therefore, it is important for the team to first identify and synchronize key yearly goals for the classroom. The purpose of agreeing on goals is to move the collective effort towards the same direction and to motivate each participant to care for the target as their own. When each player truly cares about the vision, it matters little who originated it. What matters is that the team sees the vision and wants to create it.[11] In so doing, the team members will likely develop stronger relationships and connections, and thereby positively influence students to thrive and flourish.

Aligning the group's goals and objectives with the vision for the future is considered one of the most important components in increasing employees' productivity (Cato, 2012[12]; Bryson, 1995[13]; Nanus, 1992[14]). The following case study demonstrates how shared goals and vision can transcend individual differences and enable a team to appreciate diversity rather than allow it to become an obstacle to building trust.

CASE STUDY: Lean In

From the beginning, they recognized that they were polar opposites: Beth greeted her students with a big hug as they entered the classroom. Meanwhile, Kate sat alone at her desk in the back of the room as she carefully outlined the lessons for the day and double checked that she had all the worksheets photocopied. In addition, they taught the most difficult class they had ever encountered: half of the class needed close monitoring and body regulation support, several were diagnosed with ADHD, and two were identified on the autism spectrum after neuropsychological evaluations.

Such a wide discrepancy between the educators could easily ensue disaster. However, working with Kate unexpectedly proved to be Beth's most successful co-teaching experience to date. Kate (who is nearly 20 years senior to Beth and has earned business degrees from two Ivy League schools) prefers a skills-based instructional style to Beth's outside-the-box approach. Nonetheless, Beth and Kate learned to collaborate well with each other because they agreed on one thing: they wanted engaged students. Aligning on their expressed goals of creating an inclusive classroom where children are eager to contribute their ideas throughout the school day and exhibit an insatiable appetite for learning, propelled their work forward. Moreover, what kept them afloat was that they valued each other's strengths while supporting each other's growth areas.

When Beth came up with an idea to transform their first grade classroom into a giant cave for their social studies introduction into hunter-gatherer communities, Kate did not sit on the sidelines because it was someone else's idea or complain that it would take multiple hours to tape large sheets of brown construction paper on the walls. Instead, Kate voluntarily arrived to school two hours earlier on the day of their cave construction and drafted a blueprint for the structure. She believed that the cave would thrill and inspire their students and joked about doing acrobatics at her age as she reached high to tape the paper onto the ceiling.

The cave brought their lesson alive as the children wanted to work, play, and dream under the brown-paper construction all day long. Beth and Kate grew closer as they tag-teamed, joked, and spent hours creating, decorating, and delighting their students with the joys of learning about an ancient world. Their differences became mere shadows under their co-constructed cave.

The team's goals will serve as the guiding North Star and motivate each team member to direct their individual work towards the group's aims. In turn, it will likely generate results that exceed expectations and inspire greater development of trust. Here are five strategies to facilitate the identification and alignment of goals.

TARGET EXERCISES

Target Exercise 1: Value Sort Cards

It helps to be aware of the values one upholds that shape the decisions and choices made. It is also insightful to understand your partner's core values to better empathize with their choices. Furthermore, this exercise reveals how you and your partner may align or differ on values and how to approach those differences.

Since the Value Sort Cards exercise is designed to increase self-awareness as well as deepen understanding of team members, it provides a fun activity to do with your partner(s) within the first few days of working together.

1. Each person takes eight index cards or Post-It notes.

2. On each card, write down a value you aim to create in your classroom (e.g., safety, wisdom, humor, innovation, compassion, critical thinking).

3. Each participant arranges their eight value cards, on their own, in the order of importance: The most valuable card is placed at the top of the column and the least important one is positioned at the bottom.

4. Compare and discuss your value list with your partner(s).

   a. Identify areas of alignment. Which values appear near the top of the list?

   b. Identify areas of significant difference. Which values appear near the bottom of the list? For example, does your most important value appear near the bottom of your partner's column or does it not even make their list?

5. Next, imagine that an adversity comes your way and you must now eliminate three cards from your list. Which values are eliminated and why? Which three cards does your partner eliminate? Discuss the similarities and differences.

6. Identify the three cards that you refuse to give up. Explain your choices to your team. What are your partner's three core cards? Are there similarities? How do you reconcile the differences in values with your teammates?

7. The next challenge is to flip all eight cards over with the blank side facing up so you cannot see the written contents of the cards. Shuffle the cards and then form one stack.

8. Until this step, you have been able to choose your values. This time, you have no choice over the selection process. Each participant randomly chooses three cards from their own stack (with the blank side facing up). You must now live with the three values that were blindly chosen from the stack.

9. Flip over the cards to see which values were picked. What feelings arose for you? How do you feel about having the choice taken away from you? How will you cope with the values that were picked randomly?

10. Share with your partner which values you randomly picked. Discuss how you will align your randomly chosen values with your partner, who may have picked seemingly contrasting ones (e.g., humor and critical thinking).

11. Share your insights and self-observation with your partner.

12. After identifying each other's core values, determine your collective vision for the team by highlighting areas of shared values and priorities.

13. Reach a consensus with your teammates on six shared values to uphold in your team.

Sample Follow-up Discussion Questions:

- What was it like to not have a choice in picking your values?
- What was your reaction when you and your co-teacher misaligned in values?
- How did your team align on core values?
- Were you tempted to alter your rankings once you saw your partner's lists?
- How will you negotiate the differences in values in a practical and positive way?

The random value card selection portion of the exercise is designed to help participants recognize that they can align with any value their partner chooses. In other words, one can easily learn to reframe, refine, and reprioritize one's values to establish common ground with their teammate. Therefore, differing values can co-exist within a team without causing a problem or distrust.

The Value Sort Cards, adapted from an exercise by *Six Seconds, The Emotional Intelligence Network*, can be applied in other domains, such as learning goals and assessment. For example, do this exercise with parents at a back-to-school night to further align the school community. Furthermore, this exercise can be done with the entire class, such as identifying the type of culture the students wish to create for their school year. In allowing the students to co-create their classroom culture, they will be more inclined to hold themselves accountable to uphold the collective values.

Target Exercise 2: Roles & Responsibilities Organizer

At the beginning of the year, meet with your teaching team to discuss the division of workload for operating the class. To simplify this task, below is a sample worksheet to complete together to clearly identify and distribute the work. This sample graphic organizer can be easily adjusted to address the tasks appropriate for your team.

To have the roles and responsibilities clearly mapped out and agreed upon at the beginning of the year will contribute significantly to creating a highly effective and efficient team. It will also help to minimize, although not eliminate, future misunderstanding and miscommunication.

Responsibility	Time	Name(s)	Notes
Curriculum			
Identify curriculum goals			
Plan curriculum and instructional materials			
Gather supplies			
Communication			
Communicate class curriculum updates			
Maintain home contact and communication			

Responsibility	Time	Name(s)	Notes
Instruction			
Organize instructional materials			
Deliver content			
Establish classroom management plan			
Teach behavior guidelines			
Provide individual assistance to students			
Assessment			
Verify attendance			
Collect data on student performance			
Establish assessment plans			
Compile contextual notes to learning updates			
Document (e.g. photos, video), curate, share, and store students' works			

Target Exercise 3: Communication Contract

As George Bernard Shaw astutely stated, "The single biggest problem in communication is the illusion that it has taken place." When opinions vary, stakes are high, and emotions run rampant, it is easy for misunderstanding to escalate and cause unnecessary pain. Therefore, it is extremely valuable to establish agreed-upon guidelines to help you steer the conversation and minimize conflict. Despite its value, it is very rare for teaching teams to co-create communication guidelines. Instead, co-workers simply assume and hope that their partner will act respectfully and professionally.

All communication should strive to ensure safety (e.g., emotionally, psychologically, physically) for all parties involved. The best way to achieve that is to co-create and sign a communication contract that the team agrees to honor.

Here are three steps to begin the process:

1. Brainstorm specific actions you will always keep in mind while communicating with each other. For example, be polite, be specific, be concise in your opinions, and ask clarifying questions rather than make assumptions.

2. Brainstorm barriers to effective communication. For example, fixated on being right, being judgmental, yelling, avoiding responsibility, and blaming others.

3. Commit to regularly review the communication contract (e.g., weekly, monthly, quarterly). Without consistent recommitment and practice, the agreement will eventually be forgotten.

Here is a sample communication contract to get you started.

1. We will see each other as a valuable source of insight and expertise.

2. We will treat each other in a respectful manner at all times. This means following the accepted rules of politeness (e.g., saying please, thank you) and no name-calling.

3. We will always bring any issue or disagreement with each other first before going to anyone else.

4. We will bring all questions and/or concerns directly to the pertinent individual(s) within 24 to 48 hours to try to resolve it. It is assumed that items not addressed within this time frame are not crucial or will be forgiven.

5. We will begin the dialogue with forgiveness to assure continued communication.

6. We will not assume that silence means agreement; question silence. And question assumptions.

7. We will always give feedback using the following format: Begin with two positives and then one recommendation.

8. We will always be willing to admit an error, apologize, and make a new commitment.

9. Use "I" statements. We will always speak from our own perspective and avoid using "you" statements, which generate guilt and blame. For example, use this template:

I feel _____ when _____. I need _____.

10. We will identify any aspect(s) of the conversation that we want to keep confidential. And if we are asked to keep something confidential, we will honor the request.

Operating from a shared communication contract will deepen your understanding of your teammate, facilitate a supportive and constructive environment, and multiply your ability be effective. Be sure to periodically review the communication contract to keep it current and encourage its practice.

Target Exercise 4: Tri-Arc Exercise

Our brain readily responds to visual stimuli. Therefore, creating a vision board that represents your team's objectives and occupies a prominent spot in the classroom is invaluable. Co-create a vision board for the team together using the following steps:

1. Take a sheet of paper (e.g., 8" x 11"), position it horizontally, and fold it into thirds.

2. Title the first column, "Where are we now?" Draw symbolic images or texts that represent the current state of the team.

3. Title the third column, "Where do we want to go?" Draw symbolic images or list text that reflect the ideal vision for the team.

4. Title the second/middle column, "How are we going to get there?" Make a list of goals, steps, resources, emotional states, and so forth needed to reach your big vision. See the sample below.

Step 1: Where Are We Now?	Step 3: How Are We Going to Get There?	Step 2: Where Do We Want to Go?

In co-creating the Tri-Arc Map together, striving for and maintaining the team goals become a collective effort. It is important to track the group's progress throughout the year in order to actualize the shared vision in the third column. One way to do this is to assess the team's achievement of the goals listed in the second column during the weekly team meeting. Remember to stay positive during the assessment.

A similar activity can be done with the students where each child contributes one image or a word for the classroom's collective vision board.

Target Exercise 5: Ball Balance

Once the team goals have been established, a fun game to demonstrate the impact of aligning to the group's target is the ball balance exercise. Three tools are required for this exercise:

- Large key rings (approximately two inches in diameter and found at a local hardware store). Each team needs one key ring.

- Ball of yarn or strings. Each string needs to measure at least 4 feet long to ensure that the exercise is challenging.

- Tennis balls. Each team needs one ball.

The object of the game is for each team to balance a ball on the key ring to the finish line by only holding onto the ends of the strings, which are tied to the ring.

Version A

1. Tie four-foot-long, or longer, pieces of yarn onto one large key ring. It is usually four pieces of yarn tied to a key ring. However, if there are three members to a team, you can tie only three pieces of yarn. If there are only two members to a team, each person can hold onto two pieces of yarn so four pieces of yarn are attached to one key ring.

2. Make a start and finish line that are at least ten feet apart.

3. Each team gets a ball and a key ring with strings attached.

4. Balance a tennis ball on a key ring.

5. Each team member stands up and pulls onto one end of the yarn so that the tension of the strings balances the ball on the key ring.

6. The team must walk or run from the start to the finish line without dropping the ball. If the ball drops at any time before reaching the finish line, the team must return to the start line and begin again.

7. The team(s) has 5 minutes to reach the finish line.

This game can be modified to accommodate the team's size and the physical space available.

Discussion Questions:

- To achieve the team's end goal, what became the area(s) of focus? How did you contribute to the team's efforts?

- What adjustments did you need to make to better align with your team?

- Imagine how difficult the task would be if you had to pull all the strings yourself.

If your team is already collaborative and aligned, this exercise may be too easy. If that is the case, try Version B of this game.

Version B (Ball Balance Gone Rogue)

Version B is the same setup as version A, but this time, each team member chooses a different finish line without informing others. The key is to keep your end goal hidden from your teammates.

1. Each team begins at the same start line.

2. This time, each player chooses a finish line in their own mind (different from the one used in version A) and does not reveal the location to the other members of one's team. That is, each player only knows their own finish line and no one else's. As a result, team members may move in opposite directions.

3. The team(s) has 5 minutes to reach one of the finish line(s) of their choosing, without disclosing the location of the finish line(s) to their teammates prior to reaching it.

Discussion Questions:

- Were you able to reach your goal?

- How did it feel when your teammate's end goal was unknown to you?

- What happened when each player pulled the strings in different and unexpected directions?

- How did you feel about your teammate during the game?

- What assumptions and beliefs did you create about your teammate during the game?

Once a goal is clear and shared, it seems to take less effort, yet inspire greater productivity to achieve the desired results. When members of the team uphold opposing or diverging goals and neglect to express them, it is highly unlikely that the group will achieve success despite much effort.

PITFALL: [D]EFY

Disagreements are inevitable in team endeavors. *How* the team handles disagreements is the litmus test for the emotional and social health of the group. If team members respectfully listen and empathize with differing points of view, the disagreement is likely to be resolved and it may further motivate the group to arrive at innovative and actionable solutions. In navigating complex dilemmas in education and classroom behavior management, there is definitely more than one valid solution available. Therefore, it is important to approach a problem from multiple angles, consider many options, and compromise to arrive at solutions that work for all of those involved.

In contrast, if a disagreement provokes a person to defy their co-worker by resisting or challenging their partner's ideas, which they label as inferior, the individual becomes more invested in defending their own viewpoint and could care more about being right while making the other person wrong. Consequently, this response creates an adversarial dynamic, which could prompt the other teammate to also become entrenched in their own views and exhibit similar defensive behavior. In so doing, a verbal tug-of-war ensues and the mind becomes closed off to the other's perspective in favor of defending one's position. As a result, this oppositional stance makes it very difficult to arrive at a solution that would satisfy both parties involved.

CASE STUDY: Bridging the Great Divide

"Don't touch me!", "What's wrong with you!", and "Gross, get away from me!" are common outbursts from the middle school students in Michael and Emily's class. Managing their students' behavior as their hormones rage and their bodies undergo growth spurts has been the teachers' most difficult task. Michael wanted to get ahead of the problem and adamantly pushed for an authoritarian approach of expecting the students to follow the rules set by adults, without question. He adheres to the adage that the teacher knows what is best for the child. Emily opposed his behavioral control approach that relied on expectations of obedience and punishment as a consequence. She favored restorative practices where the students take responsibility for their self-regulation and self-monitoring and have the opportunity to take action to repair a break in their relationships. Moreover, she wanted the students to participate in devising the classroom behavior agreements.

Their philosophical differences came to a head when a group of students began to poke and prod each other in a game of pretend tasing (adopted from the game of tag) based on police officers' use of taser guns. This aggressive and startling game made kids feel unsafe during recess. Emily led a classroom discussion on appropriate touching and the students expressed their opinions on how to create a safe space during recess. Although tasing stopped during recess, soon thereafter, the students began disrupting the class when they morphed their game — a student initiates a hug and then sneak attacks with a pretend taser instead.

Michael immediately wanted to institute a no touching and no hugging rule. He believed that it is the adult's job to set clear boundaries and hold the students accountable to a written rule. He feared that if students were given leeway in making decisions with their teachers regarding classroom conduct, chaos would ensue and the students would take over the classroom. Furthermore, he believed that the teachers needed to help the students redirect their focus to learning core skills and stop wasting time talking about behavior management.

Emily refused to implement a no touching rule since she enjoyed hugging students to make them feel safe or appreciated. She believed that the real problem was the unsafe game, not hugging. She sought out opportunities to foster open dialogue with the students because she believed these incidents were rich social and emotional learning moments where students could wrestle with their own values, beliefs, and relationship with others.

The teachers' misalignment left the students confused so they continued their inappropriate interactions, which alerted the principal. The principal listened to each teacher's perspective on discipline and classroom management and recognized that they both made valid points that could be fused together into a joint plan. Like Michael, the principal believed that the teachers need to stick to a plan that spells out the behavior expectations and holds students accountable with consequences. She also saw the value in Emily's approach to first include the students in the conversation to help them better understand the purpose of the ground rules and to include their input into the plan so that they could feel more ownership and motivation in maintaining a safe environment. Recognizing and incorporating elements from both Michael and Emily's playbooks generated a behavior policy that proved to be far more effective than either of the teacher's plan alone.

DEFY REMEDIES

When you notice a cycle of defiance among teammates, stop. Take a break and observe yourself and your tendency to react to the situation in order to make a more thoughtful and reflective choice. Then try any one of the following strategies to deliberately break the cycle of defiance and rebuild rapport with your partner.

Defy Remedy 1: Humor

Prepare jokes to share with your teammates. These jokes should not involve hurtful sarcasm or ridicule and all teammates need to be in on the joke. If the joking is one-sided rather than mutual, it undermines trust.

When used in a positive way that does not cover up painful emotions, laughter reduces stress and tension, brings people closer together, and generates intimacy. It is a powerful tool to smooth over disagreements and build rapport. Humor can quickly transform a disagreement into an opportunity for shared play and fun. It can also inspire creative problem-solving and help reframe disputes that may otherwise seem bleak.

Defy Remedy 2: Ask Clarifying Questions

If you disagree with your partner's perspective, rather than negate it, try to understand it by asking clarifying questions, such as the following:

- *Can you tell me more about...?*
- *Can you give me more details or examples?*
- *What are your main concerns?*
- *What do you see as an obstacle?*

By focusing on better comprehending your partner's position rather than disputing it, you will foster connection and compassion.

Defy Remedy 3: Validate with "Yes, And" Statement

Disagreements can often be diffused by hearing and validating your partner's perspective. Rather than respond defensively, validate your partner(s) by making a "Yes, and" statement and avoid a "Yes, but." "Yes, and" is a response practice and a theater exercise from improvisational comedy that requires a person to accept what another participant has stated ("yes") and then add onto that line of thought ("and") rather than subtract or negate it ("but"). In so doing, you validate your partner and encourage a collaborative process. Essentially, join in rather than negate.

Example:

> Teacher A: For our unit on Mayan civilization, let's have the students plant corn in the school garden.

> Teacher B: Yes, and we can have the students wear Mayan work clothing, which I can make, while they garden.

> Teacher A: Great, and let's give a writing assignment about their experience and the science behind the Mayan agriculture system.

> Teacher B: Sure, and some students can write a skit about the Mayan culture.

> Teacher A: Wonderful, and the students can perform the skit to the parents at the Back-to-School Night.

Defy Remedy 4: Perspective-taking Exercise

When you are in the midst of a disagreement, rather than remain stuck in your position, consider differing perspectives and recognize that there are multiple solutions and techniques to solve a problem. One way to do this is to put yourself in the shoes of your partner by taking the following steps:

> 1. Like an actor playing a character, replay or describe the conflict solely from your partner's point-of-view.

> 2. Replay the conflict until you reach an understanding of your partner and their position, which you did not previously realize.

3. Move forward with empathy for your partner.

Once empathy is established, disagreements tend to be more productive and team members appear as a resource rather than an opponent. Moreover, before initiating an important discussion, imagine being on the receiving end of that communication so that you act and speak with compassion for the listener.

Defy Remedy 5: Importance Rating Scale

Disagreements are inevitable in teamwork. However, it may not always be productive or efficient to discuss each issue. Therefore, it helps to assess how important a particular issue is to each team member in order to clarify how to move forward.

1. Each team member gauges how important a dispute is to them on a scale of 1-10: 1 is negligible and 10 is a deal breaker.

2. The partner with the significantly lower rating surrenders their position. Your team decides what constitutes a "significantly" lower rating (e.g., 3 points of difference).

3. If both parties assess a similar rating for their positions, keep discussing the issue until the rating adjusts to a 3-5 range of difference.

For instance, your team disagrees on how to start the morning meeting. You prefer to begin with joke-telling, whereas your partner wants to do an academic review of the previous day's lesson. To resolve this dispute, each team member rates on a scale from 1 to 10 the importance of the morning meeting practice (joke-telling versus academic review). If you decide it is an 8 but your partner rates it a 4, then your teammate can decide to let you start the day with joke-telling since it is significantly more important to you. However, if you rate this as an 8 and your partner decides that it is a 7, then continue discussing the pros and cons of this issue until you arrive at a solution where both parties feel satisfied or until someone changes their rating so that there is a significant gap between the two. Remember to decide in advance, prior to assigning the rating, what constitutes a significant gap in the scores (e.g., 3 or more).

In sum, the majority of the work needed to reach a team's vision involves alignment. Once your team truly aligns on shared goals, reaching the target becomes more achievable as members gauge their own actions in terms of service to the group and at the same time accept team decisions and tasks as if they are their own. (The Ball Balance game demonstrates this phenomenon.) In so doing, the collective effort builds trust and moves the group forward in the same direction, resulting in outcomes that may exceed your expectations. So the next time you find yourself in a conflict, ask if it is more important to defy your partner or focused on getting aligned so that you can move forward towards achieving your vision and remarkable results.

Teamwork is the ability to work together toward a common vision. The ability to direct individual accomplishments toward organizational objectives. It is the fuel that allows common people to attain uncommon results.

—Andrew Carnegie

CHAPTER 2

RECOGNIZE

The most basic of all human needs is the need to understand and be understood. The best way to understand people is to listen to them. —Ralph G. Nichols

To further align the team, it is important to look at similarities and differences in one's own and one's partner's patterns of thoughts, feelings, and actions. In so doing, there is a tendency to highlight disparities or attribute causes to problems. However, it is more important to magnify agreements because that facilitates progress and moves the team forward.

When noticing the differences, appreciate them as they help to diversify and challenge assumptions, inspire innovation, and expand perspective. Take time to recognize how the team members' contrasting viewpoints may complement rather than hinder the group. Moreover, identify potential obstacles that may arise due to the discrepancies so that the team can devise plans to tackle the challenges when they arise.

Self-Awareness

To identify the team's similarities and differences, the first step is to take a hard and honest look at oneself. It is vital that we examine ourselves and understand our strengths, growth areas, triggers, blind spots, vulnerabilities, and especially parts of ourselves that we are afraid to confront or try to ignore. If self-awareness is not developed among the team members, the culture created within the group will likely reflect the unfavorable characteristics that are repressed or ignored.

Recognizing one's automatic, recurring patterns of thoughts, feelings, and actions is the crucial step to managing one's reactions. Once the pattern is identified, then one can make a conscious choice on how to best respond. Determining one's patterns also helps one to take full responsibility for one's emotions and actions, rather than blame others.

Record Yourself

One of the most effective ways to pinpoint patterns of thoughts, feelings, and actions is to videotape oneself teaching. Although it can be very uncomfortable and vulnerable to observe oneself in action, it provides invaluable feedback that tends to motivate growth. For instance, Fred was a confident ESL teacher who received positive feedback from his managers. However, when he watched a video of his instruction, he was shocked. He was surprised to observe that he spoke too fast, which makes it very difficult for his students to follow and understand him. He felt sorry for his students, angry with himself for being insensitive, and regretful for being unaware of his speech pattern.

To get to the root of the problem, he decided to record a conversation with his friends. When listening to the recording,

Fred realized that his native English-speaking friends spoke at a similar speed as he did. But in class, he recognized that he spoke at an even faster rate.

Fred reviewed the video again to look for clues in his rapid-fire speech and noticed a string of anxious behaviors: he wrung his hands, fidgeted ceaselessly with his pen, paced back and forth, and often scratched his neck, and ran his fingers through his hair. This set of unconscious actions was unique to his pattern in the classroom. Thus, he recognized that his quick speech was probably a byproduct of his core underlying problem — anxiety stemming from being a new teacher.

He resolved to calm himself down before teaching. He switched from drinking coffee to tea, completed his preparation the night before his class, and rehearsed his instruction in front of a mirror prior to delivery. Soon thereafter, his nerves settled and the speed of his speaking — now a major focus of his development as a teacher — gradually reduced. Regular reviewing of his teaching videos helped him to track his progress.

Fred's students received the benefits of his changes as he purposely slowed down and frequently checked in to verify they were understanding him. In turn, his students were less stressed and perplexed when following his instruction, which ultimately created a more relaxed and enjoyable classroom environment.

Most classrooms are not equipped with a video camera and it can be difficult to solicit feedback from colleagues for classroom instruction due to any number of reasons and restrictions, such as lack of time. Therefore, the exercises in this chapter are designed to facilitate and enhance self-observation, self-analysis, and self-awareness skills.

Once self-awareness is heightened, it is easier to clearly, empathically, and more "objectively" recognize a teammate's typical emotional responses and behaviors, and thereby better understand them. The goal is to first develop self-knowledge. Then observe and validate one's partner's patterns to minimize projection and blame, as well as develop empathy. This objective can be enhanced by improving observation skills.

CASE STUDY: Tracking Tangents

Mary keeps her paperwork organized and prepared, an expression of her Type A personality. It was a surprise when she chose to co-teach with Kevin, who is impulsive and gets easily sidetracked by different interesting topics. Although Mary enjoys seeing the students energized by Kevin's suggestions, she gets frustrated with his unfiltered comments that tend to drive the students in new directions, which may not always be conducive to the day's learning goals and planned curriculum. Even though Kevin recognizes that his comments may be off topic, he cannot seem to help himself.

Not wanting to squelch Kevin's drive and noticing that his infectious enthusiasm endears him to the students, Mary came up with a thoughtful solution that honors his passion for tangential thinking but also keeps him focused on the day's lesson. Rather than censor him and impose her more methodical delivery approach, she enlisted the help of their students. Kevin loved this solution because it helped him to further develop his relationship with the children.

Mary assigned two students each day to act as the "tangential police." Each time Kevin and anyone else wandered off topic, the students would signal an agreed upon gesture to remind him to get back on track. "The students came up with it themselves," Kevin said. "It was a big 'T' symbol, held up in the air, made with two hands, so that I could see it."

Frequent but gentle reminders about his tangential discussions proved to be far more productive than an uncomfortable lecture by Mary, who needed him to control his off-task behavior. The students learned to quickly recognize Kevin's habit and reacted accordingly. Consequently, he was made aware of it in a supportive way and could bring himself back on track. "It never felt like a rebuke," he shared, "just a friendly nudge in the right direction."

This innovative solution to include students as fellow problem-solvers exemplifies how an unproductive habit, which could have become an awkward issue to resolve between the co-teachers, could be transformed through awareness, respectful collaboration, and a willingness to try something new.

[R]ECOGNIZE EXERCISES

To arrive at a place of respecting and valuing a teammate's response patterns, use listening to connect and empathize. Ask questions and make yourself vulnerable to truly get to know one another and become familiar with each other's beliefs, motivations, drives, and triggers.

Recognize Exercise 1: Connective Listening Exercise

One of the most sincere forms of respect is actually listening to what another has to say. - Bryant McGill

Effective communication is based on our ability to listen. However, we often hear but do not listen to each other. Listening is a foundational skill that regularly gets lost in the chaos of the day. Therefore, we are highlighting ways to improve listening to genuinely connect with one another.

Find a quiet place where you can talk with your teammate(s) without interruption or distraction. Invite your partner to share what is on their mind. As they speak, try to follow the steps below. It is not necessary to do every step. However, the more steps you do, the more effective your listening will likely be.

1. *Paraphrase.* Once your partner has finished expressing a thought, paraphrase what they said. Paraphrasing verifies that you understand and demonstrates that you are paying attention. Helpful ways to paraphrase include:

> *What I hear you saying is...*
> *It sounds like...*
> *And, if I understand you correctly...*

2. *Ask questions.* When appropriate, use questions to encourage the speaker to elaborate on their thoughts and feelings. Avoid making assumptions about the other's intentions. Instead, ask questions to clarify their meaning, such as the following:

> *When you say _____, do you mean _____? How so?*

3. *Express empathy.* Prioritize validating feelings, even negative ones, to avoid judging or opposing the other person. For example, if the speaker expresses anger, rather

than react to it, consider why they feel angry, regardless of whether you think that response is justified. Another person's emotion feels just as real and true as yours, and therefore, it is important to acknowledge it.

Here is one way to respond: *I can understand how that situation could make you feel (words expressed by your partner) .*

4. *Use engaged body language.* Show that you are engaged by making eye contact, nodding, facing the other person, and maintaining an open and relaxed body posture. Be aware that certain body gestures can communicate something completely opposite from your intention, such as the folding of your arms, which often signifies close-mindedness or resistance.

5. *Avoid judgment.* Your objective is to recognize and understand the other person's perspective and acknowledge it, even if you may disagree. Do not interrupt with counterpoints or mentally prepare a rebuttal while the other person is speaking.

6. *Avoid giving advice.* The objective is to understand each other's viewpoints first. Problem-solving and giving advice when it is requested are likely to be more effective after both parties understand each other's perspectives and feel heard.

7. *Take turns speaking.* After one person has expressed their views and you have engaged in connective listening, ask if it is okay for you to share your point-of-view. When sharing your outlook, express yourself as clearly as possible using "I"

statements. For example, "I feel upset when you move ahead with a parent conference plan without consulting me first."

If relevant, it may help to express empathy for your partner's attitude. For instance, "I know you feel overwhelmed and need to get work done as fast as possible so you can leave work in time to pick up your kids." Demonstrating genuine empathy can break down barriers and encourage a culture of understanding and compassion.

Recognize Exercise 2: Teacher Questionnaire

Building on psychologist Arthur Aron's research on accelerating intimacy between two strangers by having them ask each other specific series of personal questions, we developed an education-related questionnaire that can be used with your teaching partner(s). The questions are designed to promote sustained, reciprocal, and escalate personal, but appropriate self-disclosure. Subsequently, mutual vulnerability fosters closeness.

Set aside one hour or more to answer the following questions with each other. This activity can be sedentary or conducted while walking. The task of the speaker is to be honest and vulnerable. The job of the listener is to maintain eye contact, pay attention with focus and sincere interest, and find intriguing aspects of your partner's responses. Feel free to ask an appropriate follow up question if you feel inspired to do so during the conversation.

- Take four minutes and tell your partner your life story on how you got into teaching, in as much detail as possible.

- What would constitute a great classroom day for you?
- What is your most treasured teaching memory?
- What about teaching creates the most stress for you?
- Describe a difficult teaching moment for you and what you learned from that experience.
- If you could gain one teaching quality or skill, what would it be?
- What do you value most in teaching?
- What do you value most in a teammate?
- What do you bring to the teaching team?
- How do you want to check in with your teammate?
- What is your biggest concern about teaching in teams?
- What are your pet peeves in working relationships in the classroom?
- How do you want to be acknowledged when you are successful?
- How do you want feedback delivered to you?
- Complete this sentence, "I want my team to know..."
- Complete this sentence, "My team does not know..."
- Write down three things you and your partner(s) appear to have in common and then exchange your answers to see how many match.
- Share three positive characteristics about your teammate. Alternate between each share.
- Make three statements you agree on creating in your teaching team. For example, "We both want to create a learning environment where...." Write down the ones you like and keep them as a reminder of your mutual agreement.

- Make three statements you agree on regarding communication with each other. For example, "We will both ask for help...." Write down the ones you like and keep them as a mutual agreement.
- How are you most misunderstood in your communication?
- What three things do you need to feel in order to believe that you can trust your team teacher(s). Write down the ones you like and keep them as a reminder of your mutual agreement.
- What is the biggest life change you are currently undergoing that might impact your teaching?
- What are you most grateful for in your life?
- Is there something that you have dreamed of doing for a long time but have not? What stopped you from doing it.

Recognize Exercise 3: Emoji Explainer

A fun way to interpret your partner's communication style and fine-tune your decoding skills is to translate a sentence constructed in emojis by your teammate.

1. Using a smartphone, Partner A creates a sentence using only emojis.

2. Partner B translates the emojis into a complete sentence.

3. Partner A corrects or congratulates Partner B on their translation.

4. Switch roles.

Recognize Exercise 4: SWOT Analysis

To recognize your own patterns as well as your teammate's, perform a SWOT analysis on yourself and one on your partnership. SWOT is an acronym for Strengths, Weaknesses, Opportunities, and Threats. Strengths refer to actions you or your team can perform effectively as well as your or your team's experiences and skills. Weaknesses are areas to improve or possibly need to avoid. Opportunities may include new trends, changes in policy, and advancements in technology. Threats are potential obstacles and problems.

This is a technique often used to analyze an organization, business, or a department. It is a brainstorm activity that is done spontaneously with your team, without preparation.

Strengths	Weaknesses	Opportunities	Threats

Individual SWOT

1. Each team member uses the same aforementioned steps to assess oneself individually.

2. Teammates compare individual SWOTs.

3. Make a commitment to change a specific pattern of behavior that does not serve you.

4. Create a check-in calendar with your teammate(s) to follow up on transforming an unproductive behavior.

Team SWOT

1. Brainstorm with your partner(s) on each area of SWOT for your teaching team. For a larger team SWOT (e.g., all the teachers in your grade level), you can use the wall or a big poster board and write one item on a post-it note and stick it under one of the four categories. Keep adding items to each category.

2. Synthesize the data and decide which items to leverage. That is, choose a strength to amplify, one weakness to improve, an opportunity to seize, and a threat to eliminate by addressing a weakness.

3. Schedule a check-in to assess the team's growth on the SWOT analysis. This is an important step to facilitate growth and it is not to be skipped.

Recognize Exercise 5: Toss Game

This game easily yet powerfully encapsulates how communication is delivered to another person.

1. Perform this game sitting down.

2. Toss different weighted objects (e.g., book, stuffed animal, baseball) to your partner.

3. Alternate throwing, one person at a time.

4. Take turns throwing two objects in quick succession, one item with each hand, while the other player catches.

Notice how you throw the object and how your partner throws the item:

- Do you throw the object in a way that ensures your partner will catch it? That is, do you wait until your partner looks at you to know that they are paying attention?

- Does the object land within easy catching range of the other person, so they do not need to exert extra effort to catch it?

- Do you throw the object too high so that it travels over your partner's head, making it difficult to catch?

- Do you throw the object too far from the person, making it impossible to catch?

Notice how you and your partner catch the item:

- Do you go out of your way to make sure you catch the item?

- Do you catch the object only when it is easy to do so and it comes directly to you because it is not worth the effort to try to catch something that is out of reach?

- Do you fear not catching the object?

- Do you blame your partner for a bad throw when you are unable to catch the item?

This toss game is a metaphor for the multiple ways in which your communication lands on the other person. For instance, does it land directly at the other person or does it fall far from the target? The exercise also exemplifies how various weighted topics need to be communicated differently to ensure that they are properly received. That is, a light topic (symbolized by a stuffed animal) may be tossed in various playful ways without harming the recipient. In contrast, a sharp matter (represented by, for example, a pair of scissors) warrants more careful attention and handling, and therefore, requires gentle delivery with detailed communication to prevent potential damage.

PITFALL: OVERLOOK

The opposite of recognizing and respecting each other's patterns is to overlook and offend your partner. This is often done unintentionally, particularly during a time constraint, mounting workload, and stress. It also occurs when there is lack of appreciation for one's teammate.

Being overlooked threatens self-esteem as rejection is considered one of the worst human experiences. An overlooked team member begins to feel invisible, ignored, and unimportant. Positive behaviors regress and negativity increases due to built-up resentment, uncertainty, and becoming more self-centered. As a result, members may vacillate between two extremes: self-doubt (e.g., "She is right; I am wrong") and self-assertion (e.g., "I am right; she is wrong").

CASE STUDY: Negative Loop

Molly, a high performing teacher who is accustomed to running her own classroom, created a pattern of calling the shots rather than consult with her mentee and junior teacher, John. She worked diligently to fine-tune her teaching craft and acted more as an individual contributor than a collaborator. When making decisions, Molly assumed her viewpoint was right due to her seniority and would often assert her decision without any input from John. From charting the schedule to designing the curriculum, John felt that his ideas were often ignored and invalidated by Molly.

John became silent during their team meetings, doubted his abilities to teach, and feared having his ideas rejected by Molly, especially in front of the students. Consequently, the senior teacher became the director and the junior teacher acted as the performer. This pattern worked until John began to feel patronized. He then decided that he wanted more autonomy, growth, and leadership opportunities.

Resentful, John complained to his supervisor, "I have ideas about how to organize our classroom, but my teammate won't listen to my ideas. She wants things done in a certain way and says my suggestions won't work. I know that I haven't been teaching as long as she has, but I don't understand why we can't try it out. If it doesn't work well, we can learn from it and then improve."

The principal chatted informally with Molly to see if she could identify the root cause of the problem. Molly spilled a flood of complaints. She was frustrated over her co-teacher's lack of contribution, felt overburdened by being the decision-maker for the class, and believed she had to overcompensate for her partner's substandard execution. She worried, "I want more time to plan and let John run the class on his own. But I'm afraid that he won't teach the way we planned, the students will be confused, and the parents will complain."

Ironically, both educators expressed similar agendas: Molly wanted John to make decisions that aligned with the classroom learning goals and confidently teach in her absence while she planned. John wanted more agency in making those decisions for the class, more freedom to teach, and try out different ideas on his own. Work was needed to better align their goals and standards through connective listening and not assuming a worst case scenario.

Rather than recognize their similarities, this team created a negative loop that broke each other's trust by overlooking each other's needs and strengths. To end this negative cycle, Molly needed to stop assuming the role of "the expert" and let go of her need to control the class, especially if she wanted more time to plan. She needed to provide John space to test out his own ideas and learn from his mistakes. If she wanted to leave the class to plan, she needed to provide John the support structures to succeed. John needed to initiate conversations with Molly on aligning both individual and team goals and standards. Once Molly had more autonomy in planning and John received more freedom to lead the class, the two were able to boost their trust, better leverage their individual strengths, and increase their opportunities for growth.

OVERLOOK REMEDIES

Overlook Remedy 1: Attitude of Gratitude

If you find yourself overlooking your teammate's needs, or your co-worker suggests that you are doing so, shift your attitude to one of gratitude. Use the following sentence template to restore trust and recognize each other's needs:

*I'm sorry, I did not intend to _____ . I did/do intend to _____ .
And I appreciate _____ .*

For example, "I'm sorry, I did not intend to make you feel like I'm offloading all my challenging tasks onto you. I do intend for us to be fair with each other in dividing up the workload. I do appreciate you bringing this to my attention because I agree that neither one of us should feel overburdened."

Overlook Remedy 2: Review Teacher Questionnaire

To enable your partner to feel heard and valued, review your teammate's relevant responses from the Teacher Questionnaire conducted during the Recognize Exercise section. If your partner's preferred ways of being heard and appreciated are unclear from the questionnaire, then simply ask your co-worker these questions:

- *How do you want to be heard?*
- *How do know when you feel heard?*
- *How do you know when you feel valued and appreciated?*
- *What specifically do you need from your teammate?*

Remedies for Being Overlooked

If you are feeling overlooked and offended by your teammate, try the following actions to balance the relationship:

1. When having a conversation, notice how long it takes before a person interrupts another. If you are frequently being interrupted during conversations, request one minute of uninterrupted time to express your thoughts.

2. Do not be afraid to toot your own horn and express your contributions to be acknowledged.

3. Identify what your teammate's needs. Not having an important need met could be the cause of them overlooking and offending you. For example, if your co-worker needs validation for a good lesson delivered but feels unappreciated, then they may react negatively and overlook you in return.

4. Ask your partner for a small favor (e.g., borrow a book) so that they can do a conscious act of kindness for you. Performing an act of kindness increases one's connection to that person. Do something nice in return.

I don't like that man. I must get to know him better.

—Abraham Lincoln

CHAPTER 3

⟦U⟧NLOCK

*Too often we underestimate the power of a touch, a smile,
a kind word, a listening ear, an honest compliment,
or the smallest act of caring, all of which have the potential
to turn a life around.*

—Leo Buscaglia

Once patterns of thoughts, feelings, and actions are recognized and understood, trust and rapport between team members strengthen. This bond provides the members the safety needed to take risks, fail forward, and co-create through collaboration. Innovation is often the result of a collaborative exchange between individuals rather than derived from a person working in isolation. For instance, Bill Gates has highlighted that "recent research suggests that creativity is less an attribute of individuals than an emergent property that bubbles up within communities of people solving problems together."[15]

To stretch the team's potential, help unlock each other's mind by approaching a problem with a growth mindset, optimism, and flexibility. *Growth mindset,* a concept developed by psychologist Carol Dweck, refers to the "belief that basic abilities can be developed through dedication and hard work"[16] rather than assuming that they are innate and fixed. Through this lens, failure is seen as a positive growth opportunity to learn from rather than a source of shame. Using the mindset, *there is no failure, only feedback,* how could problems be approached differently?

Optimism requires prioritizing the opportunity rather than the crisis of any challenge. Being flexible means being open and receptive to the ever-changing environment as well as adapting to any situation to achieve the best results.

CASE STUDY: Tune In

During Mel's first year of teaching, she was not afraid of managing all the changes that come with working in a new state or devising the curriculum for a kindergarten class, which she had never taught. What she feared most was working with another teacher in her classroom: If she failed to engage the students, will her partner think she is a boring teacher? If she was not prepared for the day's lesson, will her co-teacher be disappointed? If the students do not demonstrate that they are learning, will her teammate think she is incompetent?

On the second day of teaching, Mel felt stuck while teaching a lesson on rhythm and rhyme as her speech and movements became robotic. Her co-teacher, Ryan, interrupted and asked if he could try something different. He shared silly poems, which prompted the students to laugh loudly and break the tension. He then sang a popular name game, "Billy Billy bo-illy, banana-fana fo-fillie, fee-fy-mo-millie... Billy!" This fun game that all the kindergarteners knew allowed them to hear their own and others' names in a rhythmic way. Ryan stepping in with a silly song broke Mel's paralysis, shifted her focus from making her presentation perfect to prioritizing the students' experience and enjoyment of learning.

Later that day, Ryan and Mel laughed over the students' silly ideas for the poems. Ryan then asked a reflective question, "What was happening for you during the lesson? Is everything okay?" Rather than criticize Mel, as she had feared, he wanted to know what blocked her from being the easy-going and happy person that he knows her to be outside of the classroom. Mel admitted that she was paralyzed by her need to be perfect and her concern over the quality of the lesson. During her instruction, she panicked when she spotted one of her students having trouble focusing and another sneakily reading a book. In addition, having another teacher in the room heightened her self-criticism of her lesson and interactions with the students.

Mel realized that her fears were unfounded when Ryan's contribution to her lesson significantly added value rather than subtracted from the students' involvement and enjoyment of her teaching. Ryan inspired Mel to let go of perfectionism. Instead, he modeled being authentic and present so that Mel could better tune into the emotional climate of the class, pivot towards a creative release, and have fun with the students so they could experience the excitement of learning.

Not only did Ryan demonstrate compelling teaching in the classroom, but he brought his creative spirit to all areas of his work. When he and Mel would get stuck while crafting their curriculum, instead of forcing themselves to power through the problem, they would pause and co-create a song as Mel played the guitar and Ryan plucked the banjo. This musical break would unleash their creativity and ideas would pour out onto the blank whiteboard. Learning from Ryan how to unlock herself and others in any situation freed Mel to enjoy difficult moments while offering her best self to her team and students.

ⓤNLOCK EXERCISES

Unlock Exercise 1: "Yes, Let's"

To boost creativity and productivity, lessons from the world of improvisational comedy can help teams to take risks in a playful way, while being supportive and open to the fact that anything can happen. The central tenet of improv is "Yes, and" (discussed in Chapter 1), which entails listening fully, accepting your partner's input, and then responding by building on what is offered. The key is to not block or reject your teammate's idea.

An improv game that exemplifies this fundamental principle is "Yes, let's," which involves action and performance. "Yes, let's" helps participants warm up to the experience of accepting whatever comes their way, being flexible, and then adding to rather than subtracting from an idea. In this exercise, there are no mistakes and no failures.

1. Pick a group activity (e.g., a class fieldtrip).

2. Player A begins by saying, "Let's_____" (fill in the action). Player A acts out the activity (e.g., riding the bus).

3. Player B joins the activity by mirroring Player A's action. After completing that action, Player B then says,

"Let's_____" (proposes a different action) to advance the group activity (e.g., take selfies).

4. Both players agree loudly by saying, "Yes, let's do that" and start performing the new action.

5. Player C joins the activity. Then Player C suggests another activity to do. All the players agree loudly by saying, "Yes, let's do that," and perform the activity, and so on. This creates a train of different activities.

6. The game continues until everyone has suggested something. If there are only two members in a group, repeat the "Yes, let's" steps until each player has been able to suggest three different ideas to perform.

The objective of the game is to focus on the group's relationship and not on the actual activity. Agreement is what allows this exercise to progress. Blocking is the quickest way to disrupt the group activity.

Notice what it is like to try on an activity that you typically would not agree to do. Did it help you to springboard another idea that was unexpected? Notice what it is like to have others accept your suggestion without any resistance. Did you feel more supported by your partner than usual?

Unlock Exercise 2: Team Logo

Create an image that acts as a logo/metaphor for the ideal version of the team and hang it in the classroom as a daily visual reminder of what you are co-creating with your partner(s). This image can serve as an inspirational anchor to unlock your team's potential. For example, a bridge can represent a solid, stable, and well-functioning teaching team that allows people to move safely from one place to another.

Alternatively, you can draw a mandala. A mandala is a sacred circle that is used as a transformative tool to gain wisdom and compassion. The circle is often a symbol of connection, unity, and harmony. Awareness of a mandala has the potential to change how we see ourselves, others, and our community.

Start making a mandala by drawing a large circle on a blank paper. Inside the circle, draw whatever comes to mind related to the kind of trust the team aspires to create. To come up with an image, consider the team's commonalities, shared highest goals, strengths, and values.

Unlock Exercise 3: Animal Farm

When feeling stuck and helpless with resolving a problem, it helps to reenact the situation through a story using figurines, such as animals, to represent the players involved. By projecting the problem onto the animal figurines, it may be easier to identify, express, and process emotions and challenges since you are looking at them from a different angle. In bypassing psychological barriers to understanding and problem-solving, this exercise can bring new insight and help clarify your experience of the situation. As a result, it can help to sort out the problem and generate ideas towards a solution.

This exercise can be done alone or with your team.

1. Think about a problem where you feel stuck.

2. Lay out animal figurines or images of animals (e.g., lion, mouse, sheep, beaver, shark).

3. Assign an animal to each person involved in this problem.

4. Tell the story of the problem from your perspective, using the animals as the characters.

5. Identify the primary emotions felt by each animal.

6. Explore why each animal is feeling a particular emotion.

7. What challenge in this problem makes the animals feel helpless, if any?

8. Retell the story from another animal's perspective. Notice what happens to your own perspective in this retelling.

9. What animal do you wish to be in this situation and why?

10. What animal do you wish *not* to be in this situation and why?

11. What do you want out of the situation?

12. What do other participants want in this situation?

13. What can you do specifically to transform the situation and achieve your goal?

In one week, check in to see if you are continuing to use your new insight and skill.

PITFALL:⬚NDERMINE

Your partner will likely express differing values, beliefs, and ideas. This may lead to disapproval and weakening of the other's perspective, while inflating your own. If you undermine and undervalue your partner and their contributions, a hierarchical, superior-inferior power dynamic between teammates can ensue and quickly erode trust.

CASE STUDY: Power of Frameworks

Communicating with parents on student behavior, especially when the educators have different levels of experience, skills, and confidence is often challenging. Having completed two degrees in English, Gary comfortably communicates with parents, who are closer to his age than his junior co-worker, Mark, who is more than a decade younger and is fairly new to teaching. As a senior educator, Gary was positioned to mentor Mark.

At the beginning of the school year, the students' behavioral challenges emerged and the parents' demands for individualized attention to their children increased, which resulted in a hike in communication needs. Overwhelmed by the large range of students' behaviors, Mark communicated with anxiety when engaging in conversations with parents about the students' actions in class. Gary observed that Mark tended to report information to parents in a worried and emotionally charged manner where the parents felt blamed for their kids' misbehavior and compelled to punish them at home for their misconduct. For instance, Mark would state, "Your child hit another student when he did not get to play with the toy first. This is not safe and we can't have him lashing out at other students." Mark's alarming tone did not meet Gary's communication standard so he would interrupt the conversation and provide a more calm and neutral perspective that would encourage the parent to partner with the teachers to resolve the situation. For example, Gary would write in email communication, "It seems that your son often gets overstimulated by sound, touch, and other senses. As a result, he gets easily overwhelmed and engages in disruptive interactions with his peers when they do not respond in the manner that he expects. We are working with your child to practice self-soothing techniques, use sensory tools to calm himself down before re-engaging with his peers, and make 'I' statements to communicate his needs."

To train Mark, Gary modeled his communication style with parents and instructed him on how to speak to them in a disarming way. However, Mark had difficulty adopting Gary's model because he did not understand how to apply it to different contexts and each situation appeared unique. Mark remained confused and uncertain about Gary's approach and instead defaulted to his reactionary response to parents. Frustrated by Mark's lack of growth and fearful that he would poorly represent the team, Gary started interrupting and taking over any communication that Mark initiated with a parent. Gary also became increasingly resentful that coaching Mark consumed so much of his work time, yet it resulted in minimal progress.

Gary's distrust of Mark's abilities and undermining his efforts spread to other domains, such as curriculum development and classroom design. Gary would correct or ignore Mark's suggestions for improvement and make unilateral decisions for the team.

Feeling undermined and undervalued for his contributions, Mark complained to their vice-principal. In evaluating his challenge with parent communication and Gary's frustration with Mark's lack of improvement, their vice-principal realized that they were missing a framework and template to structure their verbal and written parent communication. Gary needed to coach his teammate, not by telling him the appropriate comments to use case-by-case, but by providing a framework that Mark could then follow independently and ultimately replicate. With input from both educators, the vice-principal created a parent communication framework that emphasized empathy and support for the student's growth areas. Then, the message template recommends to clearly identify the educators' action steps that align with the school's goal, highlight any work needed for positive behavioral conduct, and request support from parents, if necessary.

With an effective framework and template, Gary did not feel the need to police Mark's communication and was relieved to reduce his coaching time. Mark felt more independent and incrementally gained more confidence in interacting with the parents.

UNDERMINE REMEDIES

To restore trust, inquire rather than blame or dictate. Then agree on an action plan together. Here are five different ways to repair the damage for undermining your partner.

Undermine Remedy 1: Validate, Inquire, and Transform

To avoid undermining your teammate, here's a sentence template to validate, inquire, and transform the interaction:

Sounds like you're feeling _____.
Can you tell me more _____?
I wonder if we could _____.

Undermine Remedy 2: "I" Statements

Shift the focus from blaming others to taking responsibility. Assuming responsibility helps to restore your agency and control of the situation. One way to stop playing the blame game is to use "I" statements, such as this template from Chapter 1:

I feel _____ *when you* _____. *I need* _____.

Undermine Remedy 3: Self-Reflective Inventory

Conduct periodic self-reflective inventories to interrupt behavior that breaks trust. When you find yourself undermining and undervaluing your partner, ask the following questions:

- What am I afraid of? Fear is usually behind the anger that one feels when there is a disruption to achieving a goal.
- What do I need?
- What would I do if I were brave?

Undermine Remedy 4: Inspire Success

It is far more rewarding and productive to inspire success rather than punish failure. One way to do this is to emphasize "we" rather than "I" in success. Find ways to plug-in and acknowledge each other's contributions in a productive and meaningful way. Rather than focus on your partner's mistakes, find ways to give encouraging feedback to facilitate their development. To inspire a growth mindset, give feedback on demonstrated effort rather than a fixed talent. This way, your partner will stay motivated to complete a goal despite potential setbacks rather than become frustrated and quit.

Undermine Remedy 5: Positive Frame

Create a positive frame of reference for your teaching team. This can be achieved in the following ways:

- Let go of being right and making your partner wrong.

- Make the other person "good" by leading with positive intent. That is, assume that the other person is doing the best that they can and give them the benefit of doubt.

For example, if a co-worker is showing up late repeatedly, instead of labeling them as "unprofessional," consider that they are doing an extraordinary job taking care of their children on their own as a single parent prior to getting to work.

Undermine Remedy 6: TLC (Tender Loving Comment)

Find a way to publicly provide TLC (Tender Loving Comment) for your partner. For instance, give a significant compliment to your partner in a group meeting or a newsletter. You can also spread TLC about your partner to other members of your team so that it will get back to them. That is, say the TLC to one person, who then shares it with another member, and then it eventually travels to three or more people. Ask others to help forward the TLC to your partner, with the knowledge that it originated from you.

Remedies for Being Undermined

If your partner tends to undermine you, do not be afraid to give yourself credit. Be a self-validator. Here are two ways to solicit acknowledgment from your teammate and avoid being undermined.

Two Stars And a Wish

Create equality in recognition. For instance, ask for feedback using two stars and a wish feedback format. Begin by identifying two things you liked (two stars), followed by an area of growth (wish). Thus, there are more positive rather than negative comments. Here is a template for two stars and a wish:

I liked _____.
I liked _____.
I wish _____.

Bragging Session

Have a bragging session. Make a list of contributions you have made or could make in ABCP (assessment, behavior, curriculum, parent communication) or PROPS (program, routine, operations, parent relationship, social and emotional learning). Share the list with your teammate.

Undermining one's partner undercuts the team's potential. Therefore, pay close attention to how you communicate, appreciate, and collaborate with members of your team. Positive collaboration is required to leverage each other's strengths and to unlock the group's potential.

It is not blindly pushing your own agenda that will enrich the world. It is your ability and willingness to understand, appreciate, anticipate, address, serve, and support the lives of others that will.

—Rasheed Ogunlaru

CHAPTER 4

[S]UPPORT

Alone we can do so little; together we can do so much.

—Helen Keller

The success of any team is dependent on effective support between its members because the collective effort and strengths have far greater potential than an individual achievement. A demanding, multidisciplinary, and complex undertaking, such as teaching, requires a strong support system so that the burden of all the multifaceted duties does not fall solely on one individual. It is much easier to make the right decisions, improve the curriculum, and cultivate an engaging classroom culture with a supportive team behind you. That support, in essence, is embodied in the South African term *Ubuntu* — "I am what I am, because of who we all are."[17] It is recognizing that we are not just separate individuals but interdependent, such that no one wins unless all of us win.

One way to lay the groundwork for support is to prioritize relationship-building by being an advocate and foundation for each other. This can be accomplished by giving feedback in a way that facilitates the growth of others rather than shaming or criticizing. It also involves providing warmth and mutual caring for one another. In so doing, the partners will feel motivated to work hard for the team, committed to the group's success, and live up to the expectation of others.

CASE STUDY: Celebrate Success

Deb and Tracy established a weekly practice of sitting down together to write a list of the positive and negative events from their class, often times while sharing chocolate. Their lists would include students' behavior, delivery of curriculum, comprehension of the lesson, and so forth. Then they would list items that needed to be followed up with the students and the parents. Their last list was action items needed to plan ahead for upcoming curriculum, events, or school goals. Then, they would identify action items, divide the responsibilities based on their strengths and unique abilities, and set deadlines.

In co-creating the lists, each contributing her own items and thoughts, they felt they had each other's back. They did not feel alone in operating the classroom and were comforted by the fact that one would catch what the other had missed. Deb focused on big picture planning while Tracy excelled at executing the details of a lesson. In fostering a supportive "Yes, and" environment, the teachers would come to their meeting fully engaged, attentive, and confident that they would be productive. It felt as if their list was the most important thing for them to complete at the moment to meet the needs of the students and their families.

In the days after their meeting, they would share a completed task that generated good news, such as a successful parent conversation or a field trip that was secured. Each little win was celebrated with a high-five or a hug to anchor the moment. Sharing completed tasks motivated them to get the work done. Celebrating their successes increased joy and satisfaction in their relationship and ultimately their classroom community.

[S]UPPORT EXERCISES

Support Exercise 1: Override Ineffective Defaults

In Chapter 2, we explored ways to enhance self-awareness and to recognize our patterns of thoughts, feelings, and actions. Our patterns help us to navigate novel situations, accomplish tasks, and manage crises. In moments of stress, we tend to default to our patterns because that is the most efficient way we have learned to survive. However, a pattern that works in one situation may prove to be ineffective in another scenario. Therefore, it is important to develop a wide repertoire of patterns to choose from rather than fall back on a few defaults.

Our defaults have been developed over several years and are often expressed involuntarily. Thus, it takes time, awareness, and support from others to break our habits and then create new and more viable patterns. Identifying our default patterns can be overwhelming and overriding them alone do not often lead to success. Therefore, we have designed a supportive system to better manage or disrupt one's defaults and to enroll the help of others when making the necessary changes.

1. Make a list of the frequent and potentially stress-inducing incidents that make up your workday (e.g., parent-teacher

conferences, resolving conflicts with your team members, disciplining students, negotiating schedules).

2. Replay the stressful situation. Bring one situation to mind and then identify your ineffective default patterns for that scenario. Do this for each stressful situation on your list. The likely culprits will be behaviors such as interrupting, micromanaging, needing to control, becoming too aggressive or passive, jumping too quickly to conclusions, and negative bias.

3. Plan your overrides. Once you know your ineffective defaults, you can take better control of the situation and override your default with a more productive response by planning ahead before these challenging moments arise. For example, if careful listening is your goal but frequent interruption is your default, rehearse a plan for connective listening before your team meeting so you will have a better chance of overriding your automatic response.

4. Design your days. For instance, do not schedule a tough negotiation at the end of the day when your patience and self-control may be low. Shuffle your schedule so that you can face your challenging moments when you are likely to have more self-control.

5. Share your list with your teaching partner, manager, or anyone else who can provide support to help override your ineffective defaults. It may be beneficial to create a graphic organizer to track your progress, such as the table below.

Stressful Situation	Ineffective Default	Override	Support Team	Progress

Support Exercise 2: Got Your Back Pass

Each teacher gets to use six "You've Got My Back" request passes and six "I've Got Your Back" support passes per year. Each pass can be used as a special spontaneous request or gift for each other. Be reasonable in your request to avoid overburdening your teammate and building resentment. For instance, if you have used all six "You've Got My Back" request passes in four months, you may be overburdening your partner. Here are sample reasonable requests:

- I'm having surgery on Thursday, and I'm very anxious. I'd like to take off on Wednesday. Can you cover for me?

- It's my birthday in the middle of the week, and I realize it's a field trip day. But is it okay that I take that day off if I schedule a substitute?

- I have out of town guests coming for dinner. Could I leave 30 minutes early so that I can be better prepared?

If your partner agrees to take on your request, write down their gift to you on a "You've Got My Back" pass and give it to them. If you offer to support your partner in a way that goes beyond the normal team responsibility, without being asked, write down your gift on a "I've Got Your Back" pass and give it to your teammate.

Support Exercise 3: Hype APP

Be a hype APP (Available for Positive Praise) for your teammate. Comments such as, "You got this!" and "You're doing great!" could go a long way during trying times. For instance, when you notice that your team member is discouraged, notice what they are doing well in that moment and shower them with positive praise. This may seem like a small gesture but it makes a big impact on fostering a supportive team environment.

Support Exercise 4: Feedback and Feedforward

The purpose of feedback is to inspire acceptance and growth as well as to help plan for the future. It is also an opportunity for reflection and connection, so it is best done in a way that fosters safety. First, create a safe space by being transparent about the feedback process. This can be achieved by asking questions, setting the ground rules about the feedback session, and identifying the steps involved. Second, give feedback in a way that motivates the recipient to hold themselves accountable, yet still feels supported. This can be demonstrated by asking what they need, giving very specific feedback, and providing concrete suggestions. Avoid shaming, blaming, or threatening your partner in any way.

You may begin with a practice session on a neutral, insignificant topic that will not push too many buttons (e.g., how books are arranged on the shelves).

1. *Establish Safe Space.* Ask, "Would you like some feedback?" If yes, follow up with, "How would you like your feedback (e.g., spoken, written down in a list, grade, two stars and a wish)?"

2. *Supportive Feedback.* Begin by asking the person to evaluate oneself first (e.g., "How do you think the lesson worked?"). Self-evaluation encourages accountability. Then give positive feedback that focuses on a specific behavior rather than personality. Offer any concerns or suggestions you have in the form of a question, when possible. For example, "Were you aware...? What do you think about...?"

3. *Feedforward.* Set an action plan so that the recipient can take ownership of the feedback and envision a positive change in behavior and outcome in the future. That is, find ways to apply the feedback the next day, week, month, and so on.

4. *Follow up.* Check in with your partner to know how the feedback worked out. Acknowledge your partner when the feedback has been implemented effectively and demonstratively.

PITFALL: [B]ELITTLE

The opposite of support is to belittle and bully your colleague. This destructive behavior often stems from a perceived threat and the need to control the situation. Belittling team members quickly erodes trust and creates an unsafe working environment. Belittling not only harms the victim's attitudes and behaviors, but it also leads team members to react in a similar antagonistic way, and thereby creates an environment where everyone suffers.

CASE STUDY: Bullying Mentor

Chloe often worked long hours into the night to prepare creative curriculum that would meet the expectations of her visionary and senior teammate, Melissa, who upheld very high standards. Melissa refused to let Chloe use lessons from her previous schools because she believed that each lesson had to be new and current to test the limits of teaching and learning.

For a math lesson, Chloe spent all night researching the content, planning the activities, and gathering the materials needed. She was excited to introduce her lesson on commerce by asking the students to trade resources rather than money. Chloe read the directions aloud in class and passed out the resources that were drawn on paper handouts that the students then had to cut out with scissors.

Instead of being impressed, Melissa was livid that Chloe delivered what she believed to be an unimaginative and confusing lesson, especially on a day that a school board member was visiting to observe their class. She scolded Chloe for not using real materials and manipulatives to represent the resources because the drawings made her lesson abstract rather than concrete. She noted that the students were confused by the lesson directions, which resulted in disorder and misunderstanding. She berated Chloe for not thinking through the lesson because the students were unclear about how to trade and what they were expected to do after the exchange.

Chloe defended herself by emphasizing the positives and highlighted that the students remained enthusiastic throughout the lesson. Melissa countered, "But they didn't even learn anything! It was so chaotic. The directions were a mess and completely confusing." She also noted that the board member worked with a group of students to clarify and correct the lesson instructions. Melissa then explained all the ways in which she would have delivered the lesson differently from Chloe. Feeling deflated, Chloe threw up her arms and blurted out, "I can't do this anymore! I try and try but I am never good enough. I spend three or more hours each night researching, preparing each lesson, and gathering materials. I work so hard!"

Melissa took a deep breath after realizing that Chloe was feeling under attack and asked her to go for a walk. "I'm sorry to hear that you're feeling frustrated," apologized Melissa. Chloe gathered her composure and expressed her needs. "I'd like you to work with me on this because I do want to improve," responded Chloe. "I know you're a fantastic teacher. But I prefer you to demonstrate for me, in a supportive way, how you want me to deliver a lesson. If you have feedback for me after I deliver a lesson, let's set up a time to talk about it rather than criticize me when I may not be able to hear it. And please include positives in your feedback as well, not just what didn't work for you."

"Fair enough," said Melissa. "We can schedule a time to go over your lessons. It would be helpful if you could be more proactive by giving me your lesson in advance so I can give you tips beforehand. And yes, I can be clearer on my expectations."

Relieved to be mentored rather than belittled, Chloe was eager to oblige.

[B]ELITTLE REMEDIES

If you are belittling your teammate and feel like you need to take control, use some or all of the following actions:

1. Ask yourself, *Where can I take responsibility in the situation?* Owning your responsibility in the mistake tends to mitigate the impulse to blame others.

2. Take a pause and before speaking, ask yourself the following: *Is it truthful? Is it necessary? Is it kind?*

3. Think of three things about your partner for which you are grateful.

4. When you notice yourself getting angry, rather than react, do something that will break your pattern. For example, drink water to cool down. Hit the anger pause button by taking six long deep breaths. Or tell yourself something funny to relax and diffuse your anger.

5. Notice the environment and body language of your partner. If your partner is exhibiting fear or discomfort, initiate a discussion. For example, "It feels like elevator air (i.e., uncomfortable) in here. Let's talk."

6. With your partner, agree on a nonverbal signal to indicate when one feels belittled and unsafe. For example, "time-out" hand gesture can be a neutral signal to indicate a need to address the issue in a one-on-one meeting.

Remedies for Being Belittled

If you feel that you are being put down by your partner, here are some ways to disrupt the dynamic and restore safety for yourself:

1. Set clear boundaries. For example, "I don't like to be name-called, it's demeaning. If there's something you'd like to change, I'd like to hear your feedback. Please be specific, in a respectful manner."

2. Let the other person know how you need to be treated. For example, you can refer to your communication contract as a mutually agreed upon code to interact with each other.

3. Distract the person (e.g., suggest to go for a walk, get coffee).

4. Remove yourself from the situation. You are under no obligation to receive the negative treatment. For example, "I do want to solve the problem but I do need to go to the bathroom."

5. Video record the interaction. If you feel unsafe, document the interaction. Prior to recording, establish in advance that you will be recording your interactions with your partner, for instance, to make sure you get it all right.

Even very harmful behaviors, such as belittling and bullying, can be transformed into something more productive because most people do not intend to hurt their teammates.

Bringing a co-worker's belittling behavior to their attention, followed by a firm but non-aggressive conversation, and aforementioned actions will likely disrupt their destructive behavior. Then shift the attention away from the individual to the team relationship and the greater collective goal because how each member participates impacts the entire group.

The way a team plays as a whole determines its success. You may have the greatest bunch of individual stars in the world, but if they don't play together, the club won't be worth a dime.

—Babe Ruth

CHAPTER 5

[T]RANSFER

Give what you have. To someone, it may be better
than you dare to think.

—Henry Wadsworth Longfellow

In any endeavor one makes, somebody has provided support along the way. One of the critical ways to provide support is to transfer knowledge and skills. This transference of information is not only valuable for teachers, but it has also been linked with higher student academic performance. For instance, in a study by Alan Daly and colleagues (Daly, Moolenaar, Der-Martirosian, and Liou, 2014[18]) that examined the relationship between social capital of educators and student achievement, they found that "the act of reaching out to other teachers to share knowledge regarding reading comprehension was associated with higher student scores on the ELA (English Language Arts) interim assessment, even when controlling for demographics and past academic performance."

Even if an educator may be less experienced than their co-teacher, one always has something to contribute. When the team's success becomes more important than an individual's gain, transfer is a voluntary and an inevitable step to take. As eloquently stated in Saint Francis of Assisi's prayer, "It is in the giving that we receive."

CASE STUDY: When In Doubt, Test It Out

Implementing a consistent, successful method for maintaining positive student behavior is an invaluable teacher's asset. However, deciding on a classroom behavior policy can be very challenging for a team of teachers, especially when the educators take radically different approaches.

Cindy has repeatedly seen the success of extrinsic motivation throughout her thirty-year teaching career. Material offerings demonstrably encouraged positive student behavior in the moment, and therefore proved to her that this approach always works. In contrast, Julie was driven to do what she believed was best for the child's growth, even if it took more time. She would often try unconventional methods, such as giving students more responsibility and power when generating their classroom behavior and environment guidelines.

However, Cindy was resolute in her methods and often cited scholarly research to justify her extrinsic motivation claims. Julie considered Cindy's short-term, results-oriented approach to be limited and wanted to explore other ways they could encourage the students to develop maturity, self-regulation, and intrinsic motivation. After much back and forth defending their own methods on this seemingly intractable issue, Julie proposed a research project that would test both of their hypotheses and involve the students in the process.

The class was divided into two teams to test out the two motivation methods: Group A would use extrinsic motivation, such as marbles in a jar and toy rewards, to encourage desirable behavioral outcomes among the students. Group B would use intrinsic motivation, such as choice time, project-based learning, and student-teacher feedback sessions to further their growth. Each group was assigned to gather data through interviewing students and researching the pros and cons of their method. The two teams would then present their findings and debate the merits of the different approaches. At the end, the students would vote, with input from their teachers, on which method to apply in their class.

While it was clear that extrinsic motivation worked and got things done, it became apparent after a few days of implementation that the students expected to receive prizes and wanted more or better rewards. A common request asked among the students was, "Where is my prize?" Therefore, relying solely on extrinsic motivation was neither economical nor beneficial for the students' learning.

The class decided to use extrinsic motivation for simple procedures, such as lining up, manners, and daily group tasks. Intrinsic motivation would be implemented for improving creative and critical thinking, for instance, during projects-based learning.

Rather than stay stuck in their separate positions, the research project provided a structure where both the teachers and the students could listen and learn from each other's methods as well as transfer their acquired knowledge and skills.

TRANSFER EXERCISES

Transfer Exercise 1: Generosity of Spirit

To foster a generosity of giving within your team, make a daily habit of asking yourself the following three questions:

- *How can I be of service?*
- *How can I impact my teammate in a positive way?*
- *How can we lift each other up so we can both feel successful?*

Generosity tends to be contagious. By regularly setting this standard of service, other team members will likely return your contribution.

Transfer Exercise 2: Acts of Kindness

Here are several ways to transfer kindness:

1. Do three conscious acts of kindness for each other so that team members feel cared for and appreciated. People who feel cared for are more likely to engage in positive exchanges and feel more comfortable asking for help.

2. Decorate a transfer jar (e.g., mason jar adorned with puffy paint) for each other. Then write positive notes about your teammate whenever you feel moved to do so and put them in their jar. Whenever you are feeling frustrated with your job or need a boost, read the notes written by your colleagues from your own jar to brighten your mood.

3. Give your partner at least one compliment a day.

4. Before or at the beginning of the school year, write a joint letter with your partner(s) from the future on what was accomplished and co-created together as a team by the end of the school year. Sign the letter and share it with your manager (optional).

Transfer Exercise 3: Observation and Feedback

Teachers often do not receive enough observational feedback from their managers on their performance, which limits their ability to improve. Therefore, to facilitate each other's growth, take turns observing one another teaching and give specific and concrete feedback, in ways described in previous chapters (e.g., two stars and a wish format). This can be done at least once a week, if scheduling permits.

Create a feedback template to transfer knowledge and skills in an organized and systematic manner. Below is a sample to get you started. When delivering the feedback, first develop rapport by applauding all the ways the lesson went well. Follow the compliments with areas of growth to consider. When delivering notes on improvement areas, try to phrase the comments in a question format to gather more data and facilitate understanding. For example, "Can you tell me why you chose to use... ?" Also, frame observations using "I" statements, such as "I noticed..., I think..., I wonder...."

Observer: _____ Date: _____
Observed: _____ Subject: _____

Specific Areas for Feedback	Positive Notes	Growth Notes
Engagement (e.g., student interests, varied strategies and resources, emotional hooks)		
Subject Matter Delivery (e.g., organized, contextualized the lesson, knowledgeable, appropriate materials)		
Learning Experience Design (e.g., set learning goals, individualized)		
Student Learning Evaluation (e.g., guides self-assessment, pair-sharing, demonstrates learning)		
Learning Modalities Used (e.g., visual, auditory, kinesthetic)		
Student Involvement (e.g., class discussion, questions, self-reflection)		

Specific Areas for Feedback	Positive Notes	Growth Notes
Transference of Learning (e.g., applies learning to other areas, creates project from new idea)		
Facilitate Storage (e.g., exit ticket to summarize new learnings)		

Transfer Exercise 4: Time to Transfer

Schedule times to transfer knowledge and skills. For example, during each team meeting, one person prepares one effective process, technique, strategy, graphic organizer, game, or exercise to share with their co-workers. After the teacher's share, the group may then evaluate, and decide to possibly adopt it.

If there is not enough time during a team meeting to transfer knowledge and skills, then schedule a skills-sharing clinic. Setting up a clinic allows newer teachers to also participate in making meaningful contributions to the team.

Then devise a storage method of the best practices that all team members can access so that everyone can build upon their repertoire of teaching techniques. The shared items may be video clips taken from model lessons, one-page description of a tactic, or a memorable graphic that can be posted on a wall.

Transfer Exercise 5: Brain Profile

Operating a high functioning classroom requires a diverse mix of cognitive strategies. Administrators often pair educators based on their different intellectual skills, in a way that is intended to complement the team. To leverage the differences as a strength, it helps to recognize each other's potential contribution areas.

1. Identify your strengths and weaknesses in the following cognitive domains, as defined by *Six Seconds, The Emotional Intelligence Network*:

Adaptability
Collaboration
Connection
Critical Thinking
Data Mining
Design
Emotional Insight
Entrepreneurship
Focus
Imagination
Modeling
Prioritizing
Proactivity
Problem Solving
Reflection
Resilience
Risk Tolerance
Vision

2. Identify at least one strength area where you can transfer knowledge.

3. Identify at least one growth area where you wish to receive knowledge.

4. Schedule a meeting with your teammate to share your assessment.

5. Commit to support each other in at least one cognitive domain, based on your strength and growth areas.

PITFALL: ⊡RAMPLE

Due to years of experience in the classroom, teachers tend to uphold strong values and beliefs on pedagogy that solidify their conviction on what is best for the child. As their career develops, these beliefs may become more firm and may generate more confidence in what works in the complex setting of education. The stakes and risks are high when educating children so teachers tend to trust and depend on what has worked for them in the past and are skeptical of new and different methods. As a result, teachers, particularly those with more experience, may passionately assert their viewpoint and methods, and at times, trample over others' perspectives and dominate the team. However, imposing oneself, even if it comes from good intentions, erodes trust, diminishes participation, and weakens the team's overall performance.

Team teaching must work as a partnership, regardless of experience and background of the members involved, where every member is appreciated and encouraged as a valuable contributor. Focusing on the collective achievement, each participant must have the opportunity to frequently transfer knowledge and skills to the team in order to maximize the group's potential.

CASE STUDY: The Intervention

Having soldiered through half of the school year without complaining, Jennifer decided that she needed the intervention of her Head of School if she was going to continue co-teaching with Steve. Initially, she got along really well with Steve and even socialized with him after school since they had similar interests. But when things did not turn out as they planned in the classroom, Steve's temper would flare up. He would blame Jennifer and subsequently, he would make unilateral decisions without consulting her. Jennifer realized that it was his insecurities in his teaching abilities that would lead him to trample over her and take over the class. She tried to be understanding and patient to maintain peace for the sake of the students. But she became increasingly depressed and frustrated when her planned learning goals for the students would be thwarted by Steve's tendency to "wing it" and make decisions on his own in the moment, based on the current classroom situation.

Jennifer has always loved teaching, but being steamrolled by Steve drained her enthusiasm and desire to show up to school. She hated to criticize a colleague and feared approaching Steve about his dominating behavior because of his tendency to be confrontational and verbally offensive when challenged. But after mulling it over, she wrote a letter to the Head of School requesting an intervention.

When the Head of School confronted Steve with Jennifer's concern, he was taken aback and hurt by her comments. He denied her accusations of trampling and claimed that she was overstating the problem because he respects everyone equally. If he appeared stern, it was because they operate under different backgrounds and attitudes on how to handle disagreements. He asserted that he did not intend to offend Jennifer and agreed to take mandatory training to improve his conduct.

The first task was to develop a chart to organize and divide their shared roles for running the class. This way, Steve would have fewer opportunities to steamroll over Jennifer's opinions, or hurry his own plans into action before she could counter. The calendar also offered accountability, with fixed due dates for each task. Being able to schedule their future work helped both Steve and Jennifer to visualize and anticipate their challenges and prepare adequately, rather than ad-lib solutions, as had been Steve's habit.

Equally important, the two agreed to set behavioral boundaries because Steve was completely unaware of his harmful actions. Although it was very uncomfortable for Steve to hear how his comments, which he deemed as "tough love," left Jennifer feeling trampled and upset, he found the process thought-provoking and necessary to help him take responsibility for his inappropriate behavior.

With careful mediation, emphasis on their shared goal of working on behalf of the students, and re-committing to support each other to teach to their fullest, Jennifer and Steve were able to repair their working relationship and move forward.

TRAMPLE REMEDIES

If you notice or are told that you are taking over the team by dominating your partner, pause and use the following remedies.

Trample Remedy 1: Stop, Drop, and Roll

Stop trampling, drop your need to be right, and roll with your partner's idea for a while. Proceed with awareness and compassion in the following manner:

1. Be patient with your colleague. People thrive on support and fall back with negative criticism.

2. Accept that everyone has their part to contribute.

3. Recognize that not everyone works the same way as you do.

Trample Remedy 2: Equitable Division of Labor

Check the role and responsibility chart from Chapter 1 to ensure fair division of workload so that both parties can equally contribute.

Trample Remedy 3: Equitable Decision-Making

To ensure equal participation, evaluate the most recent five major decisions that the team has made by asking the following questions:

- *Who made the decision?*
- *Where did the decision-making inputs come from?*
- *What evidence was used to make the decision?*
- *Was the decision-making transparent?*
- *Was the decision-making equitable?*
- *Who did the work associated with the decision?*

For the next five significant decisions that the team needs to make, do the following:

1. Each person comes up with a proposal, backed up by evidence.

2. Make a joint decision.

3. Revisit the decision to check the effectiveness of implementing the decision.

4. If a decision was effective, evaluate what worked.

5. If a decision was ineffective, evaluate what did not work and make a new commitment to try again using a different strategy.

Trample Remedy 4: Be Open to Receive

Make it a habit to invite your teammate to contribute to your work (e.g., brainstorming, organizing, presenting). By encouraging their participation, and thereby value their contribution, you build trust.

Remedies for Being Trampled

If you feel that you are being trampled and taken over, stand up for yourself and voice your perspective in a confident yet thoughtful way.

Stand and Deliver

Here are some actions to take to help you stand and deliver:

1. Review the roles and responsibilities chart from Chapter 1 and revise, if necessary. Highlight areas where you have sole responsibility and articulate your boundaries to your partner to take ownership of your work. If needed, carve out a niche that would be solely your responsibility.

2. Offer to take on more tasks to enhance your skills and increase your confidence. When taking on a new area, be sure to properly prepare and research in order to give your best.

3. Ask for mentoring in a specific area of growth. By providing an agreed upon space for your partner to transfer knowledge and skills, you can receive the benefits of your teammate's expertise without feeling trampled.

4. Offer to mentor your co-worker in an area where you excel. Training your partner allows you to demonstrate your competency and gives you an opportunity to inspire appreciation.

5. Prepare classroom work in advance and ask for feedback on the lesson prior to presenting. Making a contribution to someone else helps to build a bond between the participants.

6. Monitor how much each partner speaks. Effective teams give each other equal amounts of time to talk, without one dominating. Share equal stage time, for example, by adding time allocation for each agenda item during team meetings.

The collective effort of the group has far greater potential than an individual achievement. Therefore, it is crucial for each member to be able to generously contribute to feel ownership of the team and participate in its success. Sharing knowledge and skills with others makes one feel like a vital member of the team.

Team player: One who unites others toward a shared destiny through sharing information and ideas, empowering others, and developing trust.

—Dennis Kinlaw

CHAPTER 6

TRUST FACTOR ASSESSMENT

A major reason capable people fail to advance,
is that they don t work well with their colleagues.

—Lee Iacocca

Now that the building blocks of TRUST (Target, Recognize, Unlock, Support, Transfer) and the DOUBT pitfalls (Defy, Overlook, Undermine, Belittle, Trample) have been established, it is time to assess the team's trust factor. To do this, each team member must participate because trust is created between individuals, not generated solely from one person. This exercise is a subjective experience since the assessment is based on honest self-report rather than any objective standard. The purpose of this exercise is to better understand and start the conversation on each other's strengths, needs, and growth areas for building trust. It is recommended to gauge and track your team trust factor at the beginning, middle, and end of the school year to document the progress.

The assessment will likely bring up blind spots, triggers, and topics that are difficult to confront. Therefore, the more honest and vulnerable you are, the more you will discover, learn, and grow from this exercise. It is also important to approach this exercise with an open mind and empathy with your partner(s) to encourage them to be vulnerable as well. Use this opportunity to begin an authentic discussion on important issues that may seem too scary or challenging to confront. Probe and ask each other follow-up questions to process past interactions and pain points (e.g., What do you attribute this score to?, I wonder what you need in order to feel...). The scores may reveal your beliefs and assumptions in relationship to others that were hidden or previously unknown.

This tool may also help to initiate a conversation on a topic that you did not realize needs to be addressed. Ultimately, this assessment serves to help you and your team improve and grow. Therefore, the results are personalized and relevant for your team only and not to be compared with another group.

Set aside at least one hour to run the assessment and discuss the results with your teammate(s). Each team member assesses themself.

Trust Factor Assessment

1. *Rate Your TRUST Factor.* Evaluate how you are creating trust in the relationship by rating yourself on a scale of 1 (least) to 10 (most) for each of the five TRUST pillars below. Assess *only yourself* in the context of the relationship being considered. Do not score your partner(s).

It is important to not overthink your rating, rather give yourself the first score that comes to mind. It should not take more than five seconds to come up with a rating, otherwise you may be overthinking it.

TRUST Pillars	Score (1 to 10)
Target – Align on key shared goals despite pedagogical and personality differences.	
Recognize – Identify and respect your and your partner's recurring patterns of thoughts, feelings, and actions.	
Unlock – Approach problems with growth mindset, optimism, and flexibility to maximize the team's potential.	
Support – Prioritize relationship-building and demonstrate care to facilitate your partner's growth.	
Transfer – Generously share knowledge and skills.	

2. *Rate Your DOUBT Factor.* Assess your tendencies to erode trust by rating yourself on a scale of 1 (least) to 10 (most) on each of the DOUBT pitfalls. Again, only score yourself and not your partner(s).

DOUBT Pitfalls	Score (1 to 10)
Defy – Dispute, resist, and defend your position by making yourself right and the other person wrong.	
Overlook – Dismiss your partner's needs and contributions.	
Undermine – Subtly disapprove of your partner's perspective and participation while inflating your own.	
Belittle – Overtly diminish your partner's value and participation to the point where your teammate feels threatened.	
Trample – Dominate and seize control of the team.	

3. *Compute Your TRUST Factor.* For each of the TRUST pillar rating, subtract its corresponding DOUBT pitfall score.

TRUST Factor	Score (-9 to 9)
Target – Defy (e.g., 8 – 2 = 6)	
Recognize – Overlook	
Unlock – Undermine	
Support – Belittle	
Transfer – Trample	

4. *Compare TRUST Scores.* Compare and contrast your TRUST factor ratings for each pillar with your teammate's scores. The purpose of this exercise is to help identify areas in the relationship that need to improve or change. Notice the following:

- Which TRUST pillars generated the highest positive scores? Celebrate your successes in those areas.

- Which pillars generated the lowest scores?

- Is there a significant gap in the scores between you and your partner(s) for any of the TRUST pillars? If so, explore what may be contributing to that difference? Review the chapter pertaining to that pillar and identify strategies for remediation.

- Did you uncover any blind spots with respect to trust?

- Schedule your next TRUST Factor Assessment to track your progress.

5. *Growth Plan.* For your growth areas, as indicated by the low scores on the TRUST pillars, review the relevant chapters. Create a plan with actionable goals to boost trust by identifying which strategies to implement. Then enroll your teammate(s) to support your plan as well as to help avoid the pitfalls. Your partner also creates a growth plan for themself using the aforementioned steps.

6. *Schedule Regular Check-ins.* It is important to regularly check-in with your partner on your trust commitments. For example, do a weekly check-in on three major goals with an accountability structure for building trust. Your check-ins can be as short as 15 minutes. Air out any unspoken needs. The key is to make this meeting focused solely on developing a trusting work relationship and not about any other topic.

Rate Partner's TRUST and DOUBT Factors (Optional)

If you deem it helpful and feel comfortable to do so, you may also rate your partner on the TRUST pillars and DOUBT pitfalls. Similarly, have your partner score you along these two scales. Again, approach the assessment with an open mind. Then compare and contrast your own ratings of yourself with your partner's scores of you, and vice versa. Consider the following:

- Look at the gaps in the scores between your self-ratings and your partner's score of you.

- Share your justifications for your ratings. Discuss and explore possible reasons for the gaps.

- Create agreements and goals in the areas that need improvement to reduce the gap.

Rating your partner and then sharing your scores with them may be tricky and provoking, especially if the foundation of trust has yet to be established. Therefore, take care to approach the discussions using "I" statements to express your own responsibility rather than assign blame. Also, focus on the purpose of this exercise, which is to shed light on any assumptions, misperceptions, and/or unexpressed concerns between you and your partner, rather than to judge or criticize each other. Being honest and vulnerable about your needs, concerns, and mistakes will leave you and your partner feeling more connected and stronger as a team.

Great teams do not hold back with one another. They are unafraid to air their dirty laundry. They admit their mistakes, their weaknesses, and their concerns without fear of reprisal.

—Patrick Lencioni

CONCLUSION

Coming together is a beginning; keeping together is progress;
working together is success.

—Henry Ford

A t the center of the word "trust" is *us*. Trust does not reside within one person but between individuals and among groups. It is the bridge that allows two or more separate individuals to come together as a unified team, strive for the shared goal, and create something anew and more innovative than could be accomplished alone. Effective teamwork begins with building trust. Therefore, it is essential to take the time and care needed to lay the solid foundation of trust from which to build the work together. The objective of this book is to equip the readers with the tools necessary to build that stable and intimate bond and avoid the pitfalls so that the collective effort will drive the team to reach its potential.

Along that journey, disagreements, and differences are inevitable. It is crucial to examine and understand the causes of the conflicts, how they affect the individuals involved and their relationship, and bridge the divides. When trust is already established, it is much easier to explore the roots of the disagreement, be vulnerable, and quickly restore the relationship before it breaks beyond repair.

Throughout the working relationship, team members may fall in and out of trust. Thus, the strategies offered in this book are not for one-time use but to be practiced on a regular basis. Like any relationship, maintenance is key. To encourage regular usage, there are handy pocket-size reference cards in Appendix A of all the TRUST pillars and their corresponding exercises as well as the DOUBT pitfalls and their remedies.

1. Cut out Sides A and B. Each card is double-sided (i.e., definition of Target on the front side of the card and Target exercises on its back).

2. Cut out each card so that it fits in a pocket or a wallet.

3. Laminate the cards.

4. Punch a hole through the pocket-size cards to carry them on a key ring so that they are held together and readily available at all times for reference.

In any project and in any relationship, trust is the medium that bonds individuals together, enables collaboration, facilitates generous sharing of ideas and skills, and generates success. Therefore, trust is the first principle to cultivate within any team. The quality and success of the team depends on it. And any act or communication either strengthens or weakens trust. By taking actions that foster trust, we give ourselves and our team the opportunity to express our best selves and exceed beyond our own expectations. It is our choice and responsibility.

APPENDIX A

SIDE A1 ....cut here...

Target Recognize Unlock Support Transfer	**TARGET** Align on key shared goals despite pedagogical and personality differences.
RECOGNIZE Identify your and your partner's recurring patterns of thoughts, feelings, and actions.	**UNLOCK** Approach problems with a growth mindset, optimism, and flexibility to maximize the team's potential.

SIDE B1

Target Exercises	Any of these acts busts trust and casts doubt in the relationship:
Value Sort Cards – align values. Roles & Responsibilities Chart – divide workload. Communication Contract – create communication guidelines. Tri-Arc Exercise – goal board with 3 columns that answer: Where are we now? Where do we want to go? How are we going to get there? Ball Balance – team balances a ball on a ring by pulling on the attached strings.	**Defy** **Overlook** **Undermine** **Belittle** **Trample**
Unlock Exercises	**Recognize Exercises**
"Yes, Let's" – improv game where everyone acts out someone's suggestion and each player takes turns to add their activity for the group to perform, and thereby creating a series of actions. Team Logo – create a visual team metaphor or mandala. Animal Farm – use figurines to reenact a situation and project one's perspective of the problem onto the characters to gain a new understanding.	Connective Listening – use tactics to genuinely listen in order to connect and empathize with another. Teacher Questionnaire – answer personal questions to accelerate bonding between teammates. Emoji Explainer – translate sentences constructed solely out of emojis. SWOT Analysis – identify team's strengths, weaknesses, opportunities and threats.

SIDE A2

[S]UPPORT	[T]RANSFER
Prioritize relationship-building and care to facilitate your partner's growth.	Generously share knowledge and skills.
[D]EFY	[O]VERLOOK
Dispute, resist, and defend your position by making yourself right and the other person wrong.	Dismiss your partner's needs and contributions.

SIDE B2

Transfer Exercises	Support Exercises
Generosity of Spirit – ask daily, "How can I be of service? How can I make a positive impact?" Acts of Kindness – ex., give daily compliments and write positive notes to drop into your partner's transfer jar. Observation and Feedback – observe your partner's teaching and give feedback using an established template. Time to Transfer – schedule times to transfer skills and knowledge.	Know Your Ineffective Defaults – list stressful situations and plan your overrides. Got Your Back Pass – trade 6 "You've Got My Back" (request) and 6 "I've Got Your Back" (support) passes. Hype APP – be a hype APP (Available for Positive Praise). Feedback and Feedforward – reflect on growth areas and create an action plan for the future.
Overlook Remedies	**Defy Remedies**
Attitude of Gratitude – ex., "I'm sorry, I did not intend to __, I do intend to __. And I appreciate ___. Review Teacher Questionnaire – examine co-worker's responses to understand how and when your partner feels heard and valued. If Being Overlooked – request uninterrupted time to speak, toot your own horn, and identify partner's needs.	Humor – use jokes to diffuse tension. Ask Clarifying Questions – ask questions to better understand rather than negate your partner's view. "Yes, And" – validate your partner's perspective with a "Yes, and" statement rather than dispute with a "Yes, but." Perspective-Taking – put yourself in your partner's shoes. Importance Rating – rate value of an issue on 1-10 scale to decide next steps.

SIDE A3

[U]NDERMINE Subtly disapprove your partner's perspective, while inflating your own.	**[B]ELITTLE** Overtly diminish your partner's value and participation to the point where the team feels threatened.
[T]RAMPLE Dominate over your partner and seize control of the team.	**TRUST FACTOR ASSESSMENT** Gauge your trust factor by rating yourself along the TRUST pillars and DOUBT pitfalls.

SIDE B3

Belittle Remedies	**Undermine Remedies**
Own Your Mistakes – ask, "Where can I take responsibility in this situation?" Think Before Speaking – ask, "Is it truthful? Is it necessary? Is it kind?" Break Angry Pattern – ex., drink water, take 6 deep breaths, and tell a joke. Nonverbal Cue - create nonverbal signal with your partner to flag distress. If Being Belittled – set clear boundaries, remove self from the situation, and video record the interaction.	Validate, Inquire, and Transform – ex., "Sounds like you're feeling ___. Can you tell me more _? I wonder if we could _? "I" Statement – take responsibility. Ex., "I feel___ when you___. I need___." Self-Reflection Inventory – ask, "What am I afraid of? What do I need? What would I do if I were brave?" Give TLC (Tender Loving Comment) If Being Undermined – ask for feedback using Two Stars and a Wish, and brag.
Trust Factor Assessment	**Trample Remedies**
1. Rate TRUST Factor – rate oneself 1 (least) to 10 (most) on 5 TRUST pillars. 2. Rate DOUBT Factor – rate oneself 1 (least) to 10 (most) on DOUBT pillars. 3. Compute Your TRUST Factor – for each TRUST pillar, subtract its corresponding DOUBT pitfall. 4. Compare TRUST Scores – compare your scores to spot weak areas. 5. Growth Plan – devise action plan to boost TRUST in your team.	Stop, Drop, and Roll – stop dominating, drop being right, and roll with your partner's ideas. Check for Equitable Division of Labor Equitable Decision-Making – evaluate last 5 key decisions and ensure inputs from all teammates moving forward. Be Open to Receive – invite co-worker to contribute to your work. If Being Trampled – ex., stand and deliver by taking on more tasks.

ACKNOWLEDGMENTS

It takes a village fueled by trust to complete a book. We are in deep gratitude to Yun Suh for helping us to organize, structure, and produce the book. We greatly appreciate the teachers in the San Francisco Bay Area for completing our surveys that informed the research for this book. Big applause to Six Seconds, The Emotional Intelligence Network, for generously sharing some of their tools. Heartfelt thanks to Noa Mendelevitch (Blue Macaroon Design) for designing our book cover. Big thanks to Marsha Rideout for her expert proofreading. Much appreciation to Susan Charles, David Rodriguez, and the Gibbons family for giving insightful feedback on our drafts.

Many thanks to you, dear reader, for recognizing that trust is essential to creating high performing teams and having the courage to transform yourself to bring out the best in your co-workers. It is our deepest hope that the lessons and strategies gleaned and practiced from *TRUST or DOUBT* will also inspire and spread to your students and communities at large.

We Welcome Your Feedback

We would love to hear from you. We aim to continuously iterate on what works in teaching teams and welcome your feedback and comments at contact@trustordoubt.com or on our Facebook page TRUST or DOUBT. Also, please visit us at www.trustordoubt.com and receive bonus materials.

NOTES

PREFACE

[1] Beninghof, A. (2012). *Co-Teaching That Works: Structures and Strategies for Maximizing Student Learning.* San Francisco, CA: Jossey-Bass.

INTRODUCTION

[2] Cottrell, C.; Neuberg, S.; and Li, N. (2007). What Do People Desire in Others? A Sociofunctional Perspective on the Importance of Different Valued Characteristics. *Journal of Personality and Social Psychology,* 92 (2), 208-231.

[3] Cuddy, Amy. (2015). *Presence: Bringing Your Boldest Self to Your Biggest Challenges.* New York: Little, Brown and Company.

[4] Golembiewski, R. and McConkie, M. (1975). The Centrality of Interpersonal Trust in Group Process. In Cary L. Cooper (ed.), *Theories of Group Processes,* chapter 7, 131-185. New York: John Wiley & Sons.

[5] Kramer, R. (1999). Trust and Distrust in Organizations: Emerging Perspectives, Enduring Questions. *Annual Review of Psychology,* 50, 569-598.

[6] Edmondson, A. (1999). Psychological Safety and Learning Behavior in Work Teams. *Administrative Science Quarterly,* 44 (2), 350-383.

[7] Duhigg, C. (2016, February 25). What Google Learned From Its Quest to Build the Perfect Team: New Research Reveals Surprising Truths About Why Some Groups Thrive and Others Falter. *New York Times Magazine*, MM20.

[8] Bryk, A.S. and Schneider, B.L. (2002). *Trust in Schools: A Core Resource for Improvement.* New York: Russell Sage Foundation Publications.

[9] Pil, F.K. and Leana, C. (2009). Applying Organizational Research to Public School Reform: The Effects of Teacher Human and Social Capital on Student Performance. *Academy of Management Journal*, 52 (6), 1101-1124.

CHAPTER 1: TARGET

[10] Hewlett, S.; Marshall, M.; and Sherbin, L. (2013, December). How Diversity Can Drive Innovation. *Harvard Business Review.* https://hbr.org/2013/12/how-diversity-can-drive-innovation.

[11] Fritz, R. (1999). *The Path of Least Resistance for Managers: Designing Organizations to Succeed.* San Francisco, CA: Berrett-Koehler.

[12] Cato, S. and Gordon, J. (2012). Relationship of the Strategic Vision Alignment to Employee Productivity and Student Enrollment. *Research in Higher Education Journal*, 15, 1-20.

[13] Bryson, J. (1995). *Strategic Planning for Public and Nonprofit Organizations.* San Francisco, CA: Jossey-Bass.

[14] Nanus, B. (1992). *Visionary Leadership: Creating a Compelling Sense of Direction For Your Organization.* San Francisco, CA: Jossey-Bass.

CHAPTER 3: UNLOCK

[15] Kim, J. (2014, May). What I Learned from Bill Gates. *Linkedin.com.*
https://www.linkedin.com/pulse/20140508125753-32702694-what-i-learned-from-bill-gates

[16] Derived from Carol Dweck's website mindsetonline.com.

CHAPTER 4: SUPPORT

[17] May, K. (2013, December). I Am, Because of You: Further Reading on Ubuntu. *TEDBlog.* http://blog.ted.com/further-reading-on-ubuntu/.

CHAPTER 5: TRANSFER

[18] Daly, A.J.; Moolenaar, N.M.; Der-Martirosian, C.; and Liou, Y.H. (2014). Accessing Capital Resources: Investigating the Effects of Teacher Human and Social Capital on Student Achievement. *Teachers College Record*, 116 (7), 1-42.

ABOUT THE AUTHOR

ANABEL L. JENSEN, Ph.D., is an award-winning teacher who has trained over 15,000 educators, students, and parents in emotional literacy. A two-time Federal Blue Ribbon winner for excellence in education, she served as the Executive Director of the Nueva School from 1983 to 1997. At Nueva, Dr. Jensen co-created the Self-Science curriculum featured in Daniel Goleman's 1995 bestselling book, *Emotional Intelligence*. She received the 2001 Keller Teaching Excellence Award from Notre Dame de Namur University and is the 2012 recipient of the California Association for the Gifted (CAG) Distinguished Service Award for outstanding contributions to the interests of gifted children. In 2015, the Silicon Valley Business Journal named her one of the top 100 Women of Influence.

Dr. Jensen is the Co-Founder and a board member of Synapse School (K-8 independent school in Menlo Park, CA) and the Co-Founder and President of Six Seconds, The Emotional Intelligence Network, which has 11 international offices and hundreds of practitioners worldwide. She is the author of numerous publications, including *Self-Science*; the *Six Seconds Emotional Intelligence Assessment* (SEI) and its *Youth Version* (SEI-YV); *Handle with Care* book, calendar, and activity kit; and *Feeling Smart*.

Dr. Jensen earned her Ph.D. from the University of California at Berkeley and a B.A. and M.Ed. from Brigham Young University. As a professor of education at the Notre Dame de Namur University, she crafts programs and mentors educators to develop an effective climate and curricula for social and emotional learning.

KATHLEEN GIBBONS, M.A., approaches education with great purpose and passion. She has served as an educator for over seventeen years in a variety of settings — an inner city charter school in Pennsylvania, rural Yupik village public school in Alaska, and private schools in the San Francisco Bay Area. Gibbons was the Founding Teacher, Director of Programs, and an Associate Head at the Synapse School in Silicon Valley, which is grounded in social-emotional, project-based, and constructivist learning. As the Founding Head of School at AltSchool, Fort Mason campus, she worked to leverage technology to personalize education and assessment for the 21st-century learners. She earned her M.A. in Educational Leadership from Mills College and a B.S. in elementary education from Elizabethtown College.

46015533R00078

Made in the USA
San Bernardino, CA
03 August 2019